Sketchbook: 2049

14th Annual Sketchbook Festival

Edited by Liam Fitzgerald

Sketchbook 2049
The 14th Annual Sketchbook Festival

Cover Design by: Drew Dir

ISBN : 978-1-312-24738-3

Content

Program A: Reflections

Program B: Echo

Welcome to the 14th Annual SKETCHBOOK Festival.

In line with Collaboraction's evolved Mission, this year's submissions were prompted to explore the most critical social issues of our times. Curator Ike Holter noticed the theme of "history repeating" in the work. We asked the question "what if history were to finally stop repeating?" What if...

...on the night before the first preview of the 14th annual SKETCHBOOK Festival, a Revolution began. What if there was a total economic collapse followed by a blackout, and we had to postpone the festival indefinitely. We covered the costumes, props, set, lighting and sound boards, and we told the artists to go and be with their families, hopefully we would all return soon to share these 17 new short plays about the most critical social issues of 2014.

And what if in 2021, after seven years of Global war, it ended and a new world-wide governing body, the Global Union, was established. The GU picked 72 Global Hubs and inventoried all global resources and began to equally distribute throughout the world. And they made oil illegal, animals sacred and started the HEFA program to provide every Human on Earth Housing, Education, Food, and Arts. What if, by 2045, poverty, famine and cancer were on the verge of elimination.

And perhaps, in 2049, the GU then sends recovery and restoration teams into buildings that had been closed since the Revolution, one of which is the Flat Iron Arts Building in Chicago, the former home of a provocative, multi-disciplinary theatre company called Collaboraction that was intent on using theatre to incite awareness and change.

Thank you for joining us and enjoy the theatrical time capsule we call The Times of Our Lives.

Anthony Moseley
Festival Director

PRODUCTION STAFF

Festival Director ANTHONY MOSELEY
Curator IKE HOLTER
Producer SARAH MOELLER
Associate Producer LIAM FITZGERALD
Set Designer ASHLEY WOODS
Lighting Designer JEFF GLASS
Sound Designer STEPHEN PTACEK
Sound Designer MIKEY MORAN
Sound Designer MATTHEW REICH
Costume Designer ELSA HILTNER
Costume Designer KATE SETZER KAMPHAUSEN
Props Designer ANGIE CAMPOS
Props Designer RACHEL WATSON
Video Designer MICHAEL SANFILL
Technical Director DAN HAYMES
Production Manager DANIELLE STACK
Stage Manager ANDREW DONNELLY
Floor Manager BRIAN FOSTER
Box Office/Dir. of Audience Services JENNY LYNN CHRISTOFFERSEN
Assistant Stage Manager JESSICA WALLING
Run Crew KATE CORNELIUS-SCHECHTER
Run Crew AMANDA RAQUEL MARTINEZ
Run Crew BILL JOHNSON

Program A: Reflections

THE SURPRISE

a one-page play
By Corey Rieger, directed by Nathan Green

CHARACTERS
Party Host
Roger
Party Guest
Ensemble (3-20 ensemble members)

ORIGINAL CAST
Nate Card (Guest of Honor),
Jeff Dolecek (Rodger),
Tanya Mounsey (Party Host),

Ensemble:
Naomi Mark, Joel Behne, Carolyn Biery, Jaclyn Whitehair, Hannah Kopen, Christine Worden, Catherine Devorak, Lauren Twombly, Gary Henderson, Daniel Malenock, Jose Nateras

Lights up on ten or so very excited people, in a living room, mingling. A cell phone rings.

PARTY HOST
Hello? Oh perfect. Thanks, Murray! He's here everybody. He's on the elevator right now, he'll be right up. Get to your positions! Hurry. Roger dear, will you hit the lights?

ROGER turns down the lights as all the people secure themselves in their hiding spots. They await anxiously. After a few moments, the GUEST OF HONOR arrives at the door and starts to unlock it.

PARTY HOST
Shhhh. Remember everybody, wait 'til he turns the lights on.

The GUEST OF HONOR opens the door and closes it again.

He sets his keys down and lets out a sigh. He sits down on the couch in the dark with his head in his hands.

Moments pass.

After a bit, he gets up lethargically and goes to the liquor cabinet. He pours himself a large amount of booze, straight, no ice, and takes it down in one pass. He slams down the glass, lets the booze settle, and slowly trudges off to his bedroom in the dark.

A beat.
ROGER
What should we—

PARTY HOST
Shhh. Just wait a minute. He'll turn the lights on, I promise.

A long pause. The sound of a gunshot comes from the bedroom.

There is no reaction. Another long pause. Awkward.

ROGER
Should we turn…
Party Host emerges from hiding spot.

PARTY HOST
Yes, Roger, you can turn the lights on.
ROGER hits the lights.

LONE PARTY GUEST
Surprise!

PARTY HOST
Nope.

Lights out.
END OF PLAY

THE DISTANCE TO THE MOON

Devised by the First Floor Theatre.

CHARACTERS
Michele
Kelsey
Owais
Antora
Micah.

ORIGINAL CAST
Michele Stine
Kelsey Shipley
Owais ahmed
Antora DeLong
Micah Figueroa

Lights up on Stage right platform

MICHELE
Why are you so distant?

KELSEY
Distant? Jesus Christ are you really/ doing this again

MICHELE
I got you a present/ and now you're—

KELSEY
yeah like a present'll—

MICHELE
what?

KELSEY
I'm sorry…

MICHELE
Fuck that you're not sorry. TALK TO ME.

KELSEY
There's nothing to say. It's just too much./

MICHELE
/I got you a present..

KELSEY
You've been gradually *pushing* me far away/--

MICHELE
/yes but its your "phases" that have been making me--

KELSEY
My phases. This is me?

MICHELE
I am slowly losing energy. I cant-

KELSEY
You can't what--

MICHELE
I can't hold onto you any longer. You're pulling away from me. The distance--

KELSEY
The distance--

MICHELE
You've been orbiting me--huddling up against me then taking flight for a while.

KELSEY
Silence.

MICHELE
At one time, you were very close to me! Your orbits worked in a different way then. You can't remember, but I can. *(flirting)* I had you on top of me all the time. You made my nights as bright as day. And on the nights when we were calm I was unable to resist your attraction.

KELSEY
(beat) How well I know!

Michele puts her hands on the boxes.

MICHELE
They reminded me of you...

KELSEY
I can't.

MICHELE
You can't what?

KELSEY
I cant d-
Michele jumps up to the box

MICHELE
No no no. Please...just....open them...for me? Please

KELSEY
It won't fix—

MICHELE
Please. Just. open them.

Nods
Music starts and Michele opens the box.

OWAIS
At one time, the Moon was very close to the Earth.
We had her on top of us all the time, that enormous Moon: when she was full -- nights as bright as day, but with a butter-colored light -- it looked as if she were going to crush us; when she was new, she rolled around the sky like a black umbrella blown by the wind; But the whole business of the Moon's phases worked in a different way then:

Both boxes closed

Because the distances from the Sun were different, and the orbits, and the angle of something or other, I forget what. Orbit? Oh elliptical, of course: for a while it would huddle against us and then it would take flight for a while.

Sea box opens

The tides, when the Moon swung closer, rose so high nobody could hold them back. There were nights when the Moon was full and very, very low, and the tide was so high that the Moon missed a ducking in the sea by a hair's-breadth.

The fish start to move

On those nights the water was very calm, so silvery it looked like mercury, and the fish in it, violet-colored, unable to resist the Moon's attraction, rose to the surface, all of them. There was always a flight of tiny creatures -- little crabs, squid, and even some weeds, light and filmy, and coral plants -- that broke from the sea and ended up on the Moon, or else they stayed in midair.
Climb up on the Moon? Of course we did. We used to go out with those little rowboats they had in those days, round and flat, made of cork.
Lights crossfade. Sound starts to fade out.
This is how we did the job:

Shadow light on.

In the boat we had a ladder.

Ladder puppet appears

From the top of the ladder, standing erect on the last rung, you could just touch the Moon if you held your arms up. I would cling first with one hand, then with both, and immediately I would feel ladder and boat drifting away from below me, and the motion of the Moon would tear me from the Earth's attraction. My cousin, the Deaf One, showed a special talent for making those leaps. Once I even thought I saw the Moon come toward him, as he held out his hands.

Shadow puppets fade away

Now, you will ask me what in the world we went up on the Moon for; I'll explain it to you. We went to collect the milk, with a big spoon and a bucket.

Spoon and bucket appear.

Moon-milk was very thick, like a kind of cream cheese. You had only to dip the spoon under the scales that covered the Moon's scabby terrain, and you brought it out filled with that precious muck. The hard part was transporting it down to the Earth. This is how we did it: we hurled each spoonful into the air with both hands, using the spoon as a catapult. The cheese flew, and if we had thrown it hard enough, it stuck to the ceiling, I mean the surface of the sea. In this operation, too, my deaf cousin displayed a special gift; with a single, sharp throw, he could send the cheese straight into a bucket we held up to him from the boat. As for me, I occasionally misfired; the contents of the spoon would fail to overcome the Moon's attraction and they would fall back into my eye.

Light cue-sudden--switching to frontlight (ish) and shadow light goes out
The sheet drops, revealing the love triangle of Owais, Antora, and Micah.

This is how the story of my love for the Captain's wife began, and my suffering.

Because it didn't take me long to realize whom the lady kept looking at insistently: and in her eyes I could read the thoughts that the deaf man's familiarity with the Moon were arousing in her; and then it was all clear to me, how the captain's wife was becoming jealous of the Moon and I was jealous of my cousin. The one who least understood all of this was my deaf cousin.

Crossfade to ladder area

The next full moon I had arranged things so it wasn't my turn to go up, I could stay in the boat with the Captain's wife. But then, as soon as my cousin had climbed the ladder, she said: "This time I want to go up there, too!" She had never gone up on the Moon. But we all started helping her so I started to rush after her.

At that moment each one's intentions were already clear. And yet I couldn't figure things out; even now I'm not sure I've interpreted it correctly. Certainly the she had for a long time been cherishing the desire to go off privately with my cousin up there, but probably she had a still more ambitious plan: she wanted the two of them to hide up there together and stay on the Moon for a month. But had he known from the beginning that the Moon's orbit was widening?

Our friends up there must have realized what was happening; in fact, they looked up at us with frightened eyes. And from their mouths and ours, at the same moment, came a cry: "The Moon's going away!" My cousin didn't seem frightened, flinging himself into his usual somersault, but this time after he had hurled himself into the air he remained suspended. He hovered a moment between Moon and Earth, upside down, then laboriously kicking his legs he headed with unusual slowness toward our planet. In a vain attempt to give her something to grasp, I held my hand out toward her. Above me the enormous lunar disk had become much smaller.

"I'm afraid," I thought, and at that moment I jumped. I held my hand out to her, and instead of coming toward me she rolled over and over, showing me first her impassive face and then her backside.

MICHELE AND OWAIS
Hold tight to me!

OWAIS
I shouted, and I was already overtaking her, entwining my limbs with hers. I didn't realize at first that I was, indeed, making her fall back on the Moon. Didn't I realize it? Or had that been my intention from the very beginning? And at that moment our embrace was broken by our fall to the Moon's surface. I raised my eyes, sure that I would see above me the native sea like an endless ceiling, and I saw it, yes, but much higher, and much more narrow, and how small the boats seemed. A sound reached me from nearby, sketching out a chord as sad as weeping.

The fall fades out. Lights change to orbit.

Michele starts to play "Harvest Moon"

A long month began. The Moon turned slowly around the Earth. I should have been happy: as I had dreamed, I was alone with her, that intimacy with the Moon I had so often envied my cousin and with her was now my exclusive prerogative, a month of days and lunar nights stretched uninterrupted before us and everything exceeded my most luminous hopes, and yet, and yet, it was, instead, exile.

Harvest Moon chorus

I thought only of Earth. It was Earth that caused each of us to be that someone he was rather than someone else; up there, wrested from the Earth, it was as if I were no longer that I, nor she that She, for me. I was eager to return to the Earth, and I trembled at the fear of having lost it. Torn from its earthly soil, my love now knew only this heart-rending nostalgia for what it lacked: a where, a surrounding, a before, and after.

Harvest moon chorus

Clair de Lune fades in. Lights focus back to Owais.

OWAIS
When the Moon had completed its circling of the planet: not even in my darkest previsions had I thought the distance would have made it so tiny. And I recognized, we both – the Captain's wife and I – recognized my cousin: it couldn't have been anyone else, he was playing his last game with the Moon, one of his tricks. He was pushing the Moon away.

MICAH
I was unable to conceive desires that went against the Moon's nature, the Moon's course and destiny and if the Moon now tended to go away from me, they I would take delight in this separation just as, till now, I had delighted in the Moon's nearness. I was helping her departure, that I wanted to show her to her more distant orbit.

ANTORA
What could I do, in the face of this? It was only at this moment that I proved my passion for the deaf man hadn't been a frivolous whim but an irrevocable vow. If what he
now loved was the distant Moon, then I too would remain distant, on the Moon.

Lights up on the two girls, embracing each other.

KELSEY
Love?

MICHELE
Yes, I know. I know.

Kelsey: sits up. Finishes dressing. Gestures to Moon box.

KELSEY
This is yours—

MICHELE
No. It was a gift.

KELSEY
But--

MICHELE
No. Remember me by it. There are new skies for you to find. Bigger orbits.

KELSEY
I will always love you. And I'll never really leave, just fly a bit further off.

MICHELE
I know.

They kiss.

MICHELE
I love you to the moon and back.

Kelsey laughs.

KELSEY
I love you more than the whole wide world.

Kelsey exits.

OWAIS
My return was sweet, my home refound, but my thoughts were filled only with grief at having lost her, and my eyes gazed at the Moon, for ever beyond my reach, as I sought her. And I saw her. She was there where I had left her. I could distinguish the shape of her bosom, her arms, her thighs, just as I remember them now, just as now, when the Moon has become that flat, remote circle, I still look for her as soon as the first sliver appears in the sky, and the more it waxes, the more clearly I imagine I can see her, her or something of her, but only her, in a hundred, a thousand different vistas, she who makes the Moon the Moon and, whenever she is full, sets the dogs to howling all night long, and me with them.

BLACKOUT

LET ME TELL YOU WHAT I SEE HERE

By Jason Gray Platt, directed by Anna Bahow

CHARACTERS

1
2
3
4
5

ORIGINAL CAST

Jose Nateras (1)
Danny Mulae (2)
Sarah Patin (3)
Alison Banowsky (4),
Gayla Loeb (5)

Text Notes
This text is (sadly) taken from actual YouTube comments.
This structure is (brazenly) taken from Beckett's *Play*.
To maintain my own guidelines of deconstructing the texts, I make liberal use of homophones (no/know, your/you're). It makes the play appear grammatically incorrect at times, but what matters is the sound.
A dash (-) means the speaker has stopped him or herself.A backslash (/) denotes a point of overlapping or interruption by the following dialogue. Text in parentheses (text) is spoken sotto voce.
All characters can be played by performers of any gender, ethnicity, age, etc.

1, 2, 3, 4, 5 on stage.

An internet-quality video is projected onto the entire stage as well as the performers.

The video is speeding through. We don't need to know what exactly the video is.

The video pauses.

Overlapping:
1
You're shit and nobody is telling you that you're shit OH I ALREADY TOLD YOU OOPS.

2
Your face makes me want to jump off a cliff and on the way down I'm going to shoot myself.

3
How can you live knowing you make this kind of crap? If you die not a single person
would miss you.

4
OHMYGOD no one cares how you feel no joke I want to put my laptop through your
fucking throat.

5
Why don't you just go take all the pills in your medicine cabinet and slash your wrists I
would love that.

CHORUS
LOL.

The video runs for five seconds.
The video pauses.

1
You're shit and nobody is telling you that you're shit OH I ALREADY TOLD YOU OOPS.

2
Your face makes me want to jump off a cliff and on the way down I'm going to shoot myself.

3
How can you live knowing you make this kind of crap? If you die not a single person would miss you.

4
OHMYGOD no one cares how you feel no joke I want to put my laptop through your fucking throat.

5
Why don't you just go take all the pills in your medicine cabinet and slash your wrists I would love that.

The video runs for five seconds.
The video pauses.

1
Oh you're already nobody oops you're shit.

2
Want to way shoot your face the jump off a cliff.

3
Not a single person this live knowing you.

4
No one cares my god feel you fucking joke.

5
I would slash your wrists want that why don't you.

4
I feel you, how

1
nobody is telling you you're

2
off on the way to

3
not knowing a single kind person.

5
I just don't want you.

3

Live? You?

4
No, your

2
going down,

1
I told

5
you why, that

1
you're nobody,

4
I want

2
to shoot

5
you just

3
knowing you.
Overlapping
1
/ Shit!
2
/ Jump!
3
/ Die!
4
/ Joke!
5
/ Go!

The video runs for five seconds.
The video pauses.
Beat.
The video runs for five seconds.
The video pauses.

4

Ohmygod.

1
You're

3
not?

2
You-

5
Just

2
a

4
joke

1
is

5
all.

3
Not

5
that

1
nobody

4
cares

3
how

1
you

4
feel,

2
I'm

5
just-

2
I'm-

4
I-

2
I'm-

4
I-

2
I'm-

3
You you died? you /

5
Don't go.

The video runs for five seconds. The video pauses.

Overlapping
1
/ I and you
2
/ I want to
3
/ If not you
4
/ I feel you
5
/ I love you

The video runs for five seconds.
The video pauses.

4
Oh,

2
and

5
I

1
told

3
you-

2
I’m

1
shit.

4
How

3
can
1
I

3
live

4
through /

3
Not knowing you.

5
Your kind.

2
Makes me want

4
to no you, feel your

2
face your

4
throat, god

5
I would love

1
telling you that I

3
miss you, knowing you.

Beat.

2
I'm

3
not

2
myself on

3
this.

1
/"You're nobody you're shit"? That –

CHORUS
/2
I
3
miss
4
you.

2
/Going to shoot myself? I'm-

CHORUS
/1
I
5
love
3

you

5
Don’t go.

1
I

3
want

2
to

4
feel

5
you, don’t go.

1
You

3
make

2
me

4
want

5
to

3
live

2
I

3
miss

4
you,

CHORUS
Don't go.

4
This comment has been removed.

1
I

5
love

3
you,

CHORUS
Don't go.

3
This comment has been removed.

1
You're?

2
I'm-

1
Already?

2
Going,

CHORUS
Don't go.

1
This comment has been removed

2
Want

5
love

2

myself

5
just

CHORUS
Don't go.

2
This comment has been removed.

5
I love you don't go.
I miss you don't go.
Don't go.
Don't go.
Don't go.

The video runs for five seconds.
The video pauses.

5
This comment as been removed.

BLACKOUT
END OF PLAY

TO THE NSA AGENTS LISTENING IN ON THIS PLAY

By Sam Graber, directed by Mary O'Connor

CHARACTERS
Actor

ORIGINAL CAST
Guest Performers

TIME
Now.

SETTING
A Stage

Lights up.
ACTOR enters, walks to downstage center

ACTOR
FUCK! YOU!

ACTORS bow, exits.
END OF PLAY.
.

ASSHOLE

A solo pieceBy Lisa Kenner Grissom, directed by Jo Catell

CHARACTER
Lena

ORIGINAL CAST
Sarah Gitenstein (Lena)

Author's Notes:
Indented and italicized dialogue indicates an enacted past event, spoken by various characters including LENA.

Other italicized or capitalized words are for emphasis which the actor can either use or disregard.
Italicized words in parentheses are actions for the actor. Otherwise, our narrator is LENA, in the present.

Character notes: Dr. Deb - loves her position of power.
Songs for actor to acquaint herself with: **Shake Your Groove Thing* by Peaches & Herb **Closing Time* by Semisonic**I Feel It All* by Feist

"Shake Your Groove Thing" plays as LENA dances in the half-light, enjoying her body. Lights gradually come up to full.

LENA

I happen to have this ass. I don't mean to be coy but we all have qualities that get us through life. You might have a gorgeous set of teeth. Flash that smile--it gets you past the velvet rope. You take it for granted.

My special something happens to be my booty. Looks good in jeans. Looks good on the dance floor. *(She grooves)* It's not just my ass, it's also my *ASSET*. And this asset is one rather important brick in a complicated wall of confidence that I've built over time. But you know how a wall is--one brick gets loose, the whole thing can fall apart.

Let me start at the beginning. Or is it the end? It's like that song (*she sings*) *"Every new beginning is like some other beginning's end. Yeah."*

It started in my 20's. Whenever I got my period, in addition to the private party for one that is PMS, I'd get these weird icky pains in my *ASSET*. At first I could handle it. A little swipe of this stuff called *Tucks* and I'd be a-ok.

A jar of Tucks appears. She looks at it lovingly, like an old friend. A projection of a magnified jar of Tucks hovers like a halo.

Tucks. The name alone made me feel safer and "tucked in" by a *Fairy Asshole Godmother*. Tucks contain *witch hazel, which* is healthy for the skin. It's *medicated*--always a good thing. And the tag line speaks to me: SOOTHS - COOLS - COMFORTS.

My *Fairy Asshole Godmother* took care of me for a while. But after a few years her magic faded and she wasn't able to make it better with one special swipe. The pains got worse to the point where I actually gave them a name --The INFERNAL ASS PAINS.

Once, I was on a date with this Dreamy Guy. It's after dinner. My apartment. We're making out and I start moaning...but it's not *that* kind of moaning--it's the INFERNAL ASS PAIN-induced moaning. Which sounds like a whimpering alien life form. I excuse myself as demurely as possible and get my ass into the bathroom. Time goes by. *Tick. Tock.* The mood is definitely altered. I hear Dreamy Guy calling:

DREAMY GUY: Hey LENA, you ok?

LENA: Yeah....just making myself all...pretty in here.

DREAMY GUY: You don't need to do a thing, baby. You were born pretty.

LENA: I'd swoon if I could. But I'm slithering on the floor like a snake trying to wriggle out of its own skin. Whispering to Jesus and I'm an atheist. *Please, dear lord Jesus, make this go away so I can have some down and dirty sex.*
Jesus did not reply. It's possible he didn't approve. I say through gritted teeth:
I'm just...freshening up a bit. It'll be worth it. I promise.

TICK. TOCK. You could hear the wand move and the window of sexual exploration closing. *Come on, ass!* Usually it takes about 15 minutes for these episodes to pass, but this time it's taking longer. I'm in a cold sweat. I make muffled cries that sound like a wounded animal.

DREAMY GUY:Open the door, LENA. You're scaring me. Do I need to call the paramedics?

LENA:He's about to call 911 which would be even more embarrassing. I crawl on the floor and unlock the door. Dreamy Guy says:

DREAMY GUY : *What's going on in here?*

LENA: Um...I have...I have a...

LENA:But I couldn't say it. I have a HEMORRHOID. Which is a universally acknowledged *Ugly Word.* I'm way too young to utter this word! Let's consult the dictionary, shall we?

Lights shift to high school fluorescent lighting.

LENA puts on a pair of librarian-style glasses.

A dictionary appears. She opens it to the appropriate page. With a pointer in hand, she pulls down an old-school projection screen with the definition projected onto it. On a small table is the anatomy of the anus. LENA, as the teacher, reads and points:

TEACHER
Hemorrhoid: 1. An itching or painful mass of dilated veins in swollen anal tissue. 2. Dilated or bulging veins of the rectum and anus, caused by increased pressure in the rectal veins.

LENA
Rectal and *Anus* are also universally acknowledged *Ugly Words.*

Lights shift back.

Dreamy Guy and I eventually went our separate ways. It wasn't because of my INFERNAL ASS PAINS. We would have broken up anyway but let's just say this *situation*...didn't help me feel intimate.
My monthly routine became INFERNAL ASS PAINS and PMS. Dancing strange dances until it would pass. Calling out to Jesus. *(palms together, praying)*

LENA
Sweet Jesus, please save me from this pain. I'll be good. I didn't know I was bad but I'll be better.

LENA
Writhing on the bed swiping Tucks or smearing Preparation H and praying for the nerve endings to calm down. When they did, I'd get on with my day and forget all about it. Until the next time. It went on like this for, like, four years. I tried to hide it and most of the time I was successful. Flash forward. I'm with my marriage-material boyfriend, an adorable guy named Jeb. This time, it's a very special episode of *Hemorrhoid of the Month.* I decided that I needed to know whether this guy has what it takes to love me--AND my ass pains. So now, once a month, Jeb either sees what I go through or hears about it.

A gentle knock.

JEB
Infernal ass pains, honey?

LENA
Yup.

JEB
Need anything honey?

LENA
I'm good!

LENA
But I wasn't. I was in so much distress that I got down on the cool tile and did some sort of Cirque de Soleil routine to try to excise the pain. *You can't live like this*, Jeb said. And he was right. So. I went to see the doctor. A female doctor because it's easier to discuss taboo topics with a woman. Because female doctors are sure to have good bedside manners.

LENA in a harsh spotlight.

LENA
Towering in her white lab coat and six-inch Jimmy Choo heels, Dr. Deb looks at my chart.

DR. DEB
Hello LENA, what can I do for you today?

LENA
Well, um. I'm experiencing these...these...

DR. DEB
Listen, LENA. I'm one of the top COLO-RECTAL surgeons in this city.

LENA
Double UGLY WORD mash-up!

DR. DEB
I talk about this all day long LENA so give it to me straight. What's up with your ass?

LENA
It hurts like a motherfucker.

DR DEB
How often?

LENA
I tell her.

DR. DEB
How painful?

LENA
I tell her.

DR. DEB
Let's have a look, shall we?

LENA
Um...we shall.

LENA
I put on one of those flimsy paper gowns, lie on my side and shimmy my ass-- *ASSET!*-- backward into Dr. Deb's face. Then an attendant comes in so now I have two strangers with surgical gloves on, poking around, my ass up in their faces. I think about puppies. And babies. And fresh-baked cookies. Then, *SNAP*. The gloves come off. And...

DR. DEB
And...you can get dressed. OK! Lena. You have an INTERNAL HEMMORRHOID

which is common. We can keep an eye on it--

LENA
But I am in SO MUCH PAIN, Dr. Deb--

DR. DEB
Or if you feel that this is impeding your life—

LENA
I pray to Jesus once a month and I'm an atheist so I would say yes--

LENA
Dr. Deb laughs. A little too much.

DR. DEB
Then we can remove it. Simple outpatient surgery. Very routine. I suggest you come in on a Friday. Take the day off and you should be back to work in no time. Connie can schedule you at reception.

LENA
And I won't have any more pain*?*

DR. DEB
Like I said, very routine. Alright LENA we'll see you real soon.

LENA
No more INFERNAL ASS PAINS?! Sign me up, Connie!

The sound of happy birds chirping.

LENA
It's the day of my scheduled surgery. Jeb asks if I need him to take me. Nah - routine outpatient surgery. I'll be fine! The doctor assured me!
I'm euphoric. I'm gonna get my *ASSET* back. I'm gonna be myself again and I won't have to pray to a God I don't believe in. I pop on the gown and happily wiggle my naked ass back in the doctor's face. I don't feel the incision. I sing to myself *"Every new beginning is like some other beginning's end. Yeah."*
All seems fine. I mean, totally uncomfortable and weird, but the local anesthesia seems to be working. I stop at the pharmacy with a little spring in my step to fill the prescription, but I doubt I'll need it. Everything's cool.
A crow caws.

Until the world stops spinning on its axis and starts moving in the other direction. Until life as I know it is over. Until I am in hell.

The lights are dim. Foreboding. Sad.

Wearing a robe, LENA pushes a crate filled with bathroom toiletries. She does not walk upright.

She holds up the items one by one, as they are projected on screen. Tucks: the pads, the cream, the travel wipes. Preparation H: the pads and the cream. Metamucil, Colace, Sitz bath salts. A variety of baby products. Gauze in an assorted shapes and sizes. Surgical tape. Scissors. Several bottles of medication.
The fluorescent light of Dr. Deb's office.

LENA
Hi...um. Connie. Can I speak to Dr. Deb please?

CONNIE
Dr. Deb is in emergency colo-rectal surgery.

LENA
I'm experiencing a lot of pain. A great deal of pain, in fact. A FUCKLOAD of pain Connie, Excuse me.

CONNIE
Are you taking the pain medication?

LENA
The pain medication makes you constipated, which makes the whole process even more painful. See the irony, Connie?

CONNIE
Let me connect you to Dr. Deb's assistant.

LENA
The attendant whose face was also up in my ass gets on the line:

ATTENDANT
This is Anthony. How can I help you?

LENA
I am in a LOT of pain over here, Anthony.

ATTENDANT
This is very routine.

LENA
But Dr. Deb didn't say anything about the constant bleeding or the intense swelling-

ATTENDANT

--Miss--

LENA
--Or the inability to move—

ATTENDANT
--Miss—

LENA
--or sit, stand, sleep, or SHIT-

ATTENDANT
MISS!

Fluorescents out.

LENA
Fucking Jeb. I love him and he had no way of knowing. Really, he didn't. But he encouraged me to have this surgery and now he's away for the weekend at some...conference. I am ALONE! Just me and my pain. I lie precariously on my side with an ice pack balanced *just so* against my ass, phone on speaker.

LENA
Jeb, you have to come back.

JEB
Honey, don't you think you're exaggerating a bit?

LENA
This smacks of the classic male point of view: women exaggerate, women get hysterical.

LENA
(hysterical) JEB--I AM NOT EXAGGERATING!!!

JEB
One day we're going to look back at this and laugh. When you no longer have those pains, you'll be glad you did this.

LENA
COME HOME OR I'LL NEVER MARRY YOU, YOU FUCKER!!!

LENA
I hang up. If he can't show up for me, then I just might call the whole thing off.

Lights shift.

LENA
Mom, Jeb and I broke up. He didn't care about my ass.

MOM
I don't understand. And I'm not sure I want to.

LENA
We're all alone in our pain Mom. Every single one of us.

MOM
You sound a little...extreme, sweetie.

LENA
I'm telling you Mother--we are all ALONE!!

LENA
Meanwhile back at the ranch...

Lights shift.

The Carmina Burana plays as LENA takes out a gigantic box of gauze pads; surgical tape, Vaseline, ice packs, etc. She performs the following actions. She cannot stand upright.

LENA
Cut pieces of surgical tape. *Squat.* Place two large pieces of gauze on each cheek. *While Squatting.* Place tape on each square of gauze and affix to each cheek. Then *walk.* Like this.

She walks hunched over, like a wounded animal.

Get ice pack from freezer.

Sit. She takes a VERY long time to sit.

Look out window. Contemplate all the things you didn't get to do in this life. Take a BB gun and kill squirrels. In your mind. Tell the dog your secrets and beg her to carry on for you. Write a will. Think about Sylvia Plath. Feel empathy. Try to pee. Ignore the blood. Eat an apple. FIBER. Try to...y'know, *go.* Cry tears that don't fall. Cry tears that do fall. Hot, salty, angry. Sit in the bathtub. For hours.

Music stops.

Now you might wonder, did the doctor lie? YES and I will tell you why. No one in their right fucking minds would get their ass operated on if she didn't lie. She'd be out of a job this fancy COLO-RECTAL surgeon in Beverly-fucking-Hills. No

Jimmy Choos for her.

All I can do is pray.

LENA
Are you there God? It's me LENA. Please save me from this pain.

LENA
Then I scream a bloodcurdling horror movie scream into a pillow.
If you've ever wondered, *how would I react if I were in mortal pain*? No matter what religion you are, even if you are an atheist--you WILL pray to God. You will cry out for him/her/it. HE might come to you in the form of a Vicodin induced delusion. SHE might come in the form of a hallucination. IT might come in the form of the internet. *(beat)* That's it--God IS the internet and the internet is GOD!! That's why it's FREE!! How come no one's figured this out? I have experienced God in the form of screen name *"Hang-in-there- 911" and "Trying-to-be-brave"*-- and so many of you. I stumble over to my computer, Google the ugly H word, and lo and behold. A BLOG. With pages and pages of raw data that my fellow troubled assholes have found as an outlet for their pain, their grief, and their disbelief.

Lights shift to the glow of a computer screen. LENA reads as she awkwardly lays on her side.

LENA
"Hang-in-there-911" writes...*Can anyone out there who has had a hemorrhoidectomy give me an idea of how long it will take to recover? It will be 4 weeks tomorrow...*

LENA
Four weeks?! I'm on day five.

HANG-IN-THERE-911
...My doctor told me I would be healed in less than two weeks but I have since learned that all surgeons LIE...

LENA
Told ya.

HANG-IN-THERE-911
I am really depressed by my rate of healing.

LENA
Really depressed you say? And why would that be? Because there is an unbelievable difference between expectation--

DR DEB
Simple out patient surgery. Very routine.

LENA

--and outcome. I'd come after you Dr. Deb, but my inflamed asshole won't let me leave my house. I continue reading. And instead of taking Vicodin, the shared pain and the communal experience starts to make me feel better. From *"Urgent-123:"*

URGENT-123

This is the single most agonizing procedure I have experienced. It can be 8 weeks or more until you stop bleeding. I'm wondering why the hell I agreed to go through with this!

LENA

This one's for Jeb who thought I was hysterical. *"Stay-Strong"*:

STAY-STRONG

As the caregiver, I'm convinced this is the most painful surgical recovery I have ever witnessed. We were up for 36 hours straight after surgery trying to ease my wife's pain. This morning she said, "This is worse than childbirth."

LENA

My internet posse was there for me. But it didn't mean that the pain didn't get the better of me at times. That I didn't reach for the Vicodin in desperate moments. Because I did. If *"Stay Strong's"* wife needed it, then I felt ok about needing it, too.

Lights shift. LENA takes a pill and slowly lowers herself into a bathtub. Soft, moody music plays.

LENA

I am in a heavy pain-filled fog. I take a pill and get into the tub. I go under water. It feels good. What if I stay here? It's not...suicide. It's comfort. Freedom from pain. Peace.

She performs the following actions.

I will myself to get out of the bathtub. I walk like an old woman. I sing from a deep place I didn't know existed:

She sings. "Nobody knows.... the trouble I've seen..."

Am I entitled to sing an old Negro Spiritual? Me, a middle-class liberal arts educated white chick? Who can I ask for permission? Maya Angelou? Oprah? Obama? I understand it now. My soul calls out:

She dances a low swaying dance.

Nobody knows, the trouble I've seen…

Ok, Lord. I'm ready. Shine the white light and I'll follow!

LENA shrieks and dances more feverishly. A Coming to Jesus dance.

Take Me Lord! Save me Lord! Take Me Lord! Save me Lord!
She falls onto the bed. High. In a dream-state...

LENA
The stabbing pain softens as the Vicodin seeps into my bloodstream. Razor blades become rose petals. The soft flesh of flowers envelope me. No more pain...I feel beautiful now.

She drifts off, talking in her sleep. A lullaby plays until—

Jeb shakes me.

JEB
LENA, wake up. You're dreaming. I had no idea it was gonna be like this, honey.

LENA
I feel soft...and melty.

JEB
I'm worried about you. I think you need to eat something.

LENA
But then I'll just have to...y'know. GO and that's like...HELL.
JEB
I'm sorry I wasn't here--

LENA
If we're gonna be together, it's all 'in sickness and in health' and if you're not up for that then--

JEB
That's what I want to talk to you about.

LENA
Then, on bended knee the guy gets down and asks me to marry him. I'm jaundiced with a couple of bloody gauze pads taped between my swollen ass cheeks and I say...yes. Ok, that's the Hollywood ending. Jeb didn't ask me to marry him right then and there. That came later. But he did profess his love. He did assure me in sickness and in health. And as my *ASSET* got better we became closer...and stronger. Who knew my INFERNAL ASS PAINS would lead me to body acceptance and intimacy after all? Weeks went by. Slowly but surely I was able to leave my Neanderthal ways behind and walk upright. Slowly but surely I didn't have to tape gauze to my ass every few hours. Slowly but surely I was able to go to the

bathroom without screaming into a pillow. *Appreciate your asshole.* It does amazing things when it works and for most of us it works all the time. It's one of those things you take for granted, right? Well don't. I'd like to take a moment of silence to appreciate my asshole. And assholes in general. Feel free to join in.

She closes her eyes. Takes a moment.

She breathes in... and out.

"Shake Your Groove Thing" plays. LENA dances, enjoying her body, as lights slowly fade to blackout.

END OF PLAY

YOUNG FATHERS

By Joel Kim Booster, directed by Chris Chmelik

CHARACTERS
Hal
Gus

ORIGINAL CAST
Ibrahim Elmourabit (Gus)
Luke Grimes (Hal)

A child cries.
Rapid knocking at a door.
Lights up.
Gus's apartment. It's a mess.
Gus, equally a mess, sits on the couch, nearly comatose.
Hal stands outside pounding on the door.

HAL
[Gus? Gus are you there?] I'm already running late. I can't be doing this again. I can hear Wally from the hall. What the fuck is going on in there? *Augustus*, open the fucking door.

Gus finally snaps out of it.
Rushes to the door.

GUS
Oh hey. You're here. You came.

HAL
Jesus Christ. You look like shit.

GUS
Thanks for coming.

Hal pushes past Gus into the apartment. It is a disaster. Dishes and trash everywhere.

HAL
Yeah, well I have like less than ten minutes or I'll be late to work, and I really can't afford to lose this job right now and— holy shit what happened here?

GUS
I haven't had much time to—

HAL
Forget it— Where's Wally?

GUS
In there.
He points Hal to the bedroom.
Hal begins to go off.
HAL
Is he okay? Is he sick?

GUS
I don't know. He just won't stop crying. I don't know what to do.

HAL
From off:
*[*Hey there big guy, oh it's okay, it's okay, uncle Hal is here now. Your favorite uncle... I'm here, I'm here, how's my Walter? Huh? How's my Wally—]

Poking his head out the door, holding a bundled baby:

Did you try anything? Or were you just hiding from him in the other room?

GUS
No, of course not. It's just, I didn't know what else to do. I tried everything. You said, you told me I could call you if there was an emergency, and he just wouldn't stop crying so I thought maybe something else was wrong. I thought about maybe taking him to the emergency room, but he wasn't running a fever and you know we're barely out of the hole with all the bills from him being born and then Julia's accident and everything—

The baby has stopped crying.

Oh thank god.

Hal comes out.

HAL
There. Okay? You have to hold him, Gus. You have to touch him and rock him and talk to him like a fucking baby, okay? I told you that you can call me, but you cannot call me every time you're not sure how to—

Beat.

HAL
Just. Give it a little time. He probably just misses his mom.

GUS
Yeah.

HAL
Okay. Well. I have to go now. Are you going to be okay? Are you eating?

Gus is not going to be okay.

HAL
Gus?

Beat.

HAL
Gus. Please don't. I can't. I can't right now, if I'm late to another shift I could lose this job, and I really can't afford to—

GUS
Breakdown. Tears. Blubbering.
I can't do this, Hal. I can't do it. I can't take care of a *baby*. Fuckin' a, I can't get him to stop crying, I can't get him to eat or sleep. I'm fucking useless, man, I wasn't supposed to— I shouldn't be here alone, I shouldn't be— he deserves better, doesn't he? He does, you can admit it. I mean. Fucking look at me.

Hal is not making eye contact.

Look at me!

HAL
I'm looking, I'm looking! Okay?

GUS
What about any of *this* says dad to you?

HAL
Nobody *looks* like a dad at first. Nobody. Jules didn't look like a mom. Okay, but you have got to pull it together for Wally, he—

GUS
Julia's mom wants to take him. She offered. They said if it was too much, they could take him back west and—

HAL
You're kidding.

GUS
I mean, it makes sense, doesn't it?

HAL
No. Absolutely it does not make sense. Jules' funeral was like a month ago— They haven't even given you a chance to— No. That evangelical piece of shit. I cannot believe that woman. You know if she takes Wally, I will never get to see him again, right? She will take him to Sunday school and it's bye bye Gay Uncle Hal. No. You cannot.

GUS
No offense, but I could give two shits about whether or not you get to be a fake uncle.

HAL
I didn't say—

GUS
I'm thinking about him. What's best for him. And I don't think it's me.

HAL
Oh please. Don't do that. You're in a rough spot, but you'll get through this. For him, you'll get through this.

GUS
Stop. Stop saying that! Stop telling me I'll get through this, like you have a fucking clue what this is like for me.

Beat.

I can't stop worrying. I can't stop thinking about him, and all the fucked up shit in this world. It's scary. You don't even understand how scary it is until you have a kid. It's like, every day you wake up and there's something new to be afraid of. Someone brings a gun onto a train and kills 33 people or a new drug comes out and it eats your face skin or another fucking war in a country *I've never even heard of.* I was scared enough when there were two of us. Now it's just me, and I'm not ready. I'm not ready.

HAL
What and you think Nancy is going to do a better job of it in Oakland?

GUS
They did with Julia. She was perfect.

HAL
She was just as fucked up as you or me. She was my best friend— God rest her soul— But she wasn't perfect. And Nancy had a lot to do with that. That's part of being a parent. Fucking your kid up.

GUS
No. It's about protecting them. From trains and the face eating drugs, and I don't know how to do that.

HAL
Protecting him? Are you fucking kidding me? What are you going to stick him in a plastic bubble and homeschool him in your one bedroom apartment for the rest of his life? Because let me tell you, I'm not sure you're the most qualified guy to be teaching the younger generation—

GUS
Fuck you.

HAL
No— fuck you! That kid doesn't need protection. He needs his fucking dad. He's going to grow up and he's going to face some fucked up shit and when he does, he's going to need someone to hold his hand and tell him that life is fucked up but we keep going anyway and then kiss him before he goes to bed at night. What he *needs* is someone to tell him that his mother was kind and kick ass and a vegetarian. And if you don't get that, then maybe you should just fucking hand him off to Jules' mom. Jesus Christ.

Beat.

I cannot fucking believe I'm having to have this conversation with you. This is not my job, do you get that? Do you understand? I am not your "sassy gay friend" that can stop his life and sweep in and try and convince you not to give your son away because you're too sad and scared to be a fucking man about it. I was your *wife's* friend and it is only out of love for her that I am even standing here right now. *We* are not friends, we are not bros. *I do not like you*. So do not call me again with this bullshit, okay? If you need someone to show you how to change his fucking diaper, or ask what temperature his formula should be or any of that shit, Google it or call up Grandma Nancy and have her book a flight out here to do it if she cares so goddamn much. Okay?

Okay?

GUS
Okay.

HAL
And you are *not* giving my nephew to Nancy, right?

GUS
No, okay?

HAL
Good.

He plops down next to Gus on the couch. Silence.

HAL
You only get one of those speeches a year. I don't have the energy anymore.

He gets up to go.
I'm really fucking late now.

GUS
You know my dad walked out on two sons by the time he was my age. Crazy to think about, right?

Hal stops.

HAL
Yeah, well. My dad had three by the time he was our age, and he never walked out on us. Doesn't mean he wasn't a shitty dad.

GUS
Thanks?

HAL
That won't be you. You're not walking out on that kid.

GUS
What if I fuck it up?

HAL
Don't.

GUS
That simple?

HAL
Hope so. Either way, I sure as hell know Nancy doesn't know either. She probably thinks she does, too. That's worse. At least you and I know we don't know what the fuck we're doing.

GUS
That's better?

HAL
Definitely.

Beat.

Have you eaten yet today?

GUS
I'm still getting through all the food people brought over after the funeral.

HAL
Fuck, Gus. That shit cannot be good by now.

GUS
Some of it is.

HAL
You're unbelievable.

Beat.

Listen, I'm going to run and get some shit from the store. You need to eat. Real food. Do me a favor and take a fucking shower while I'm gone, and throw out the rest of that food.

GUS
I thought you had to go to work.

HAL
Whatever. It's a restaurant. There are like a thousand of them. Now clean yourself up. Try not to kill Wally while I'm gone.

GUS
Thanks, Hal. Seriously. Thank you for all of —

HAL
Covering his ears.
No, no, no, no, no. We are not gonna do that. I can't hear you. No "moments." Lalalala...

This continues until he exits.
Gus gets up. He stands at the bedroom doorway, checks on Wally.
He smiles.
Lights out.

THE BIG ONE

By Idris Goodwin, directed by Marie Cisco

CHARACTERS

Vernon
Rudy

ORIGINAL CAST

Robert D. Hardaway (Vernon)
BILL JOHNSON (Rudy)

Two men, RUDY the son and VERNON the father, are watching the big game, in a living room type situation. We don't see a television but perhaps the flicker/glow and some ambient sports-telecast type sound.

Maybe there is beer, some snacks...and though the name of the team or even the sport in particular wont be revealed, they're dressed for watching sports at home. Sweats, hoodies, backward caps, socks, house shoes.
When we begin their team has just bumbled an important play which squandered their lead. Perhaps the play begins as father and son, stand watching intently, in anticipation of something positive and then

VERNON
AAAAHHHHH!!! NOOOO!!! YOU MORON!!! YOU STUPID MORON!!

Vernon plops back into his seat shaking his head
Rudy puts his hands to his face and slowly slides them down.
Then he turns to face us.

RUDY
If they win today, they'll be breaking a long tradition.
A tradition of leaving their fans standing at the altar.
I'm talking decades here of getting just close enough to shatter all the hearts.
Fans like my dad here.

VERNON
Bunch of Goddamn stupid morons!

RUDY
Amen.
The last time they won the big one he was there.
He was maybe 10 or 11.
It was all tied up, whole game, back and forth
Dad kept knockin back those Pepsi colas. See his Uncle George was the spoiling kind and whatever dad asked for George would get for him

VERNON
I mean, what're they doing?!
WHAT THE FUCK ARE YOU DOING.

RUDY
I know! God!
So it's all tied up and my Dad's young bladder is betraying him
He'd been holding it all game.
Uncle George kept asking him, "don't you need to go?"
But he didn't wanna miss anything
But finally as the game raged on he couldn't take it anymore

He was stamping his foot, he was squirming
Uncle George says, "Kid you gotta go wiz, just go"

VERNON
(standing up)
I'm going to get another one, you want one?

RUDY
Yeah, thanks Dad.

Vernon exits.

But then, just as the tiny drops of pee are making their way out of his
Urethra---we score! Big! Widen the gap
Uncle George "Now's your chance kid GO GO"
And my dad takes off to the bathroom.
There is of course a line.
Then he hears a resounding moan a sort of "oooooooo" from the crowd.
So he rushes out of the bathroom line, back to the stands
The other team had answered right back. Closed that gap. So now dad is standing in the aisles bouncing up and down as time drifts away.
He is squeezing his prick to keep from wetting his pants
There is no way he's gonna miss this because---before this, the team had never won the big one
But then all the other guys, taller adults, they also left the bathroom line and they're crowding the aisles
And my dad can't see anymore. He is trying to fight his way through the herd of Sports dudes, all trying to hold in their beer piss
10
9
8
7
He still can't see
6
5
4
Wedges and wiggles and---
3
2
Sound of applause.

In the last moment they score ---winning the big one and my father couldn't see it—all he saw was the big hemorrhoid ridden asses of the taller adults who pushed a kid out of the way to catch the last play....
But he was there.

Vernon returns and hands Rudy a beer.

VERNON
Let's see if these turds can turn it around.

In unison they crack the beers.

VERNON
You know I was there last time they won it. I told you that story right?

RUDY
Yup. You pissed your pants with excitement.

VERNON
Okay it's back on. Come on let's turn it around you fuckin bunch of shit-wits.

RUDY
My father is not a complex man, it's basically this, what you see here.
My mother almost never comes out of her room.
She makes the French onion dip and you probably can't fully tell but it's a great dip. But mostly she stays in her room.
But she listens, because she hopes that if they win the big one, maybe my father will change.

VERNON
They're gonna do it this year, Rudy
Can't you feel it?

RUDY
Absolutely

VERNON
Hey, don't screw around. They can hear that doubt. It gets in the air.

RUDY
No, I'm serious. Coach McGee

VERNON
Yup.

RUDY
The trades, the new uniform

VERNON
Uh huh, uh huh

RUDY
They been playing like I never seen

VERNON
Damn right! I been watching these guys my whole life and I never seen em play this.....
Come on! Come on! ----
YEAH!!!
YEAH!!

RUDY
It's all tied up.

Vernon is on his feet, dancing a bit, celebratory

RUDY
This happens every year.

Rudy joins Vernon and gives him five

I play along.
I cant let on how I...
I guess I should explain.
I was just flipping the channels the other day and stopped on this movie I used to love tiger Town. Came on the Disney channel. Wasn't a cartoon though, had uh, Roy what's his name from Jaws playing this aging ball player and there's this kid and his dad. Huge fans of the Detroit Tigers who suck. The kid's dad dies and just before he dies, tells him to keep believing you know, in the Detroit Tigers---So the kid starts going to tiger games and it's unbelievable right. This guys been sucking and suddenly he's knockin em out of the park. All because this kid wishes hard in the stands. This doesn't work on TV though, so Roy what's his name, strikes out at away games But his turn around inspires the rest of team and they get to the big one at the end. The kid is all set to go to the big one but of course some bullies take his ticket---so then there's this big action sequence of the kid hustling over to tiger stadium...he gets there in the bottom of the ninth, Roy what's his name is at the plate and--- Well I wont spoil it for you anyway, this movie made a light go off for me. This kid was skipping school, fighting bullies, riding on the back of buses, risking his ass for what? Belief in what? His dad on his deathbed tells him to keep being a tigers fan? What?!Really? Is this what it's all about?

VERNON
This is it Rudy.
Can you feel it?

RUDY
Every fan has that moment
It hits em
My time
My energy
My hope
My weekend afternoons. You know I read an article about football that said after the commercials, and the time outs and the fouls There's only about 10 or 15 minutes of actual playing time? Takes you all day to watch.

VERNON
This is it Rudy.
Rudy this is it.

RUDY
This man is not complex.
It's been this. Forever. Nothing else.
He's done some pretty unforgiveable shit too
In the name of this--- 7
It's fitting he love a team that just almost----
A team that just almost lives up to its promise
He has never kept any of them.

VERNON
Your mother should be watching this.
Hey, call her for me. She won't come if I call her.

RUDY
She doesn't care Dad

VERNON
I know but for this----this is epic---she'll come out for the big one.

RUDY
I don't think so.

VERNON
Come on just tell her

RUDY
She doesn't care.

VERNON
Helen! Come here you gotta see this!

RUDY
Dad.

VERNON
Helen!
Here we go son, he we go....

RUDY
Dad.

VERNON
Here we go.
Helen come on!! You're gonna miss this!

ANNOUNCER
10...9...8

VERNON
Come on.

ANNOUNCER
7.....6....

RUDY
I don't believe dad.

ANNOUNCER
5....4

VERNON
They're gonna do it!
Helen damn it!

RUDY
DAD!

ANNOUNCER
....3...

VERNON
This is it!
This is it!
Rudy exits

ANNOUNCER
2.....

VERNON
OHHHHHH!!!!!!

ANNOUNCER
1!!

VERNON
YES! YES! YES!!
Vernon drops to his knees and thanks God
Some celebration. He looks around....he's alone.
Helen!
Rudy!
He gets up....

Looks more. Accepts it. Sits back down. Picks up the remote. Shuts the TV off.
BLACKOUT

ATTIC PLAY

By Anthony Donald Kochensparger, directed by John Rooney

CHARACTERS
Nicholas
Molly

ORIGINAL CAST
Jessica Hughes (Girl)
Alex Seeley (Boy)

NICHOLAS
My father taught
me
lessons.
He was mean.
He beat me with a broom.
He was mean.
Broom
hands
choke me hard
teach me lessons.
Women wear a dress.
Boys should not be faggots.
My father talked about women
and he said they were for fucking.
Molly, she told me.
"Molly is my name."
I found you
in my attic
eating nothing.
You were beautiful and thin.
Nicholas, I said.
"Nicholas is my name."

Knock Knock Knock.

I said are you hungry.
She was nervous.
She was so so shy.
I pushed it close
backed away.
She was nervous.
I pushed it closer

Where did you come from.

Knock Knock Knock.

My father talked about
niggers and he said
that is a word I can use.
He said I could say it too
cept I had to say people
and I didn't understand.
I told her she was
beautiful

MOLLY
I was nine
ten
eleven
just a girl
when I got married.
I was nine
ten
eleven
had my wedding
in an attic.
Wore a dirty dress
that I got from my mother.
He asked me what women
were to be used for.
"Molly," I said then
"Molly is my name."
He found me
I was alone
I was hungry
I wore a dirty dress.
"Nicholas," he said,
"Nicholas is my name."

Knock Knock Knock.

He brought food for me
"To eat," he said.
It had been a while
since I got food
or home.
It'd been a while
since I'd been here.

I ate all the food.

Knock Knock Knock.

He said about his father.
He said about his lessons.
He told me that his father
hit him sometimes.
He told me that
he didn't understand.
He said that I was
beautiful

I asked her
to marry me.
I understood her
not him.
Marry me
Molly Molly
Molly
Yes.

Knock.
A knocking sound.

Under light
in the attic
I took her hand.
She wore a dirty dress
under light
from the window
moonlight coming in
I took her hand
said
Molly I take you.
She said
my name.
She took me
too.
Wife.
We kissed
and I understood
I understood better
than my father
there was a knocking.

My father talked about women

he said they were for fucking.
I asked him about women
like my mother
and he hit me.
I asked him about
who she was
where from
was she beautiful.
He hit me
broom
hands

he asked me
To be his wife.
I said, I said
I said
I said
He asked me
I said
"Yes."

Knock.
Knock Knock.

It was dark
where we were
except a small light
coming into the chapel.
My wedding.
My Nicholas.
I wore a dirty dress
he took my hand
told me
that he took me
said
Nicholas
I take you
Nicholas
Boy
He kissed me
He kissed me
He kissed kissed
kissed me
Knock Knock Knock.

He told me about lessons

and asked about fucking.
I told him I had done it
I had fucking
he said that's okay.
He understood me
I wanted
I want
To get to know him.
I asked him
about
his

choked me hard.
He didn't know anything
about you.
He wouldn't
I don't think he would've
understood.
Knock Knock.
A knocking
on the door of the attic.
"Don't be scared,"
I said.
"Don't be scared of the knocking."

You were Molly.
My wife
that I found in the attic.
You had brown hair
eyes
you were tall but you were little.
And I loved you
all my heart
and we got married.

One day he was asleep
my father
drunk
from too much drinking.
I found my mother
in a picture
in his closet hiding
like you
(like you were hiding).
The same kind of hiding
the same kind of
eyes

"Mom," I said.
"Mom," I said to the picture.
She was wearing a pretty dress.
Knock Knock.
The knocking.
Knock.
Not to worry.
Knock.

family questions.
He didn't know a thing
but he
He said.
He said he never met his
mother.
A knocking.
Knock Knock
on the door of the chapel.
"Don't be scared,"
he said,
"Don't be scared of the knocking."

Nicholas,
my boy
who brought me food
he had dark hair
nose.
He was short but older.
I think I loved him.
He was pretty.
He married me.

I asked him about
his mother
who she was
where she went.
I asked about her
to know
I wanted to know
about him.
He kept me safe.
He kissed me good.
The same kind of
kiss

familiar
familiar to me.
When I got my pretty dress
Knock Knock.
Sounds
Knock Knock
Worry

One night I was holding you
in the attic.
One night
holding you
in a dirty dress.
Held your dirty dress
in my hands
by the stain
I lifted it up
Touch.

We were a family.
Knock.

Happy.

One night I held
your dirty dress in my hands.
There was knocking
on the attic door
a knocking and I
Knock Knock Knock Knock
knew it was my Daddy
heard him
drunk and stumble
heard him
banging hard on the door
to where I was happy.

The picture of my mother
that I found
hiding just like
you were hiding
had the same eyes
had your hair
had your
face.

He sounded mad.
He sounded like
he knew you were up here
he knew you'd come back
he knew I found you.
He knew about us
he wouldn't understand
he wasn't.

One night he held me
tight coming
in our home
he held me
in my wedding dress
put his big hands
on it
held it
pulled it
Touch.

Knock Knock
Knock

Knocking on the door.

One night we were
sleeping there was a
Knock Knock Knocking
Knock Knock Knock Knock
I was scared of it
I was scared it was
His father choke hands
Knock Knock
He sounded drunk
Knock Knock
He sounded mean
He wanted to get us.

He said about a photo
of his mother
that he found
could I see it
I didn't ask
I didn't want
not want
scare

to scare him
to frighten
to scare him away.
So I just listened
and then I heard
then I heard
a loud sound.
Knock Knock Knock

Knocking Knocking
Knock Knock Knock

My father taught me lessons
choke me hard
women were for fucking
I fucked you in your dirty dress.

Grabbed it up in my hands
pulled it up
kissed her hair.
We were a family.
We got married.
Holding hands
he didn't know.
He didn't know about it.

What was he gonna
take us away
take you away
I was finally happy
Knock! Knock! Knock!

I was finally finally happy here I had my wife I had my Molly and he didn't have to understand because up here we were alone and what he said about women and rules and faggots and niggers it didn't matter didn't matter because I had this.

Knock.

Knock.

Knock.

Made me so scared.
Knock Knock Knock.

My father taught me lessons
choke me hard
women were for fucking.
He fucked me in a dirty dress
grabbed it up in his hands
pulled it up
kissed my hair

We were a family.
We got married
holding hands
he didn't know
he didn't know about it.
What was he gonna
take us away
take me away
I was finally happy.

Knock Knock Knock!

It was so noisy.

It was so so he was gonna
get us he was gonna figure
out where we were he sounded
mean he sounded familiar
a villain like my husband used to
sound. I hoped we didn't get caught
every night I prayed to God.

Knock.

Knock.

Knock.

Knock.

He was coming for us
Knock Knock Knock
Knock Knock Knock
He had found me
Big hands choke broom
Knock Knock Knock
Knock Knock Knock
What can we do
I thought I might vomit
Knock Knock Knock
I would die without her
Knock Knock Knock
Knock Knock Knock

Knock Knock Knock.

Knock Knock Knock.

Knock Knock Knock.
I knew what to do
I knew we had to
it was time
Knock Knock Knock
I grabbed her
Knock Knock Knock Knock
"Run away with me."

"Please?"

Knock Knock Knock
"Well," I said then.
Knock Knock Knock
"Really," I said then
Knock Knock

"Now."
Knock Knock
Holding
Then

Then

Knock.

Knock.

What do we do I said_
I grabbed Nicholas I said
Nicholas what do we do
Knock Knock Knock
Knock Knock Knock
What can we do I
Was so, so afraid of his father
Knock Knock Knock
Knock Knock Knock
I felt sick in my stomach
Knock Knock Knock
My prayers were never heard
Knock Knock Knock

Knock Knock Knock

Knock Knock Knock.

Knock Knock Knock.
I hoped he had a plan
Knock Knock Knock
Knock Knock Knock _
He grabbed me
Knock Knock Knock,
Looked me in the eye.
"Run away with me."

"Please?"

It got louder
Knock Knock Knock,
I said I would
Knock Knock Knock
"When?"

Knock Knock
Hands
Knock Knock

Then

The door opened
No no no no
I stood there holding her
frozen
my father finding both of us.
"Dad," I said
"This is Molly.
This is my wife.
This is who I love."
And he didn't understand.
He just kept staring
like she was something familiar.

Then

chills chills chills
he stood there staring
I stood there holding him
frozen
He looked like he could cry
Then Nicholas
started crying
I couldn't I couldn't
I was nine ten eleven
when I was married.

END OF PLAY

DREAM SCENARIO

By Ike Holter, directed by Dexter Bullard

CHARACTERS

KYLE - Black, mid twenties, smooth talker, attractive.
MARI - White, mid twenties, incredibly fast talker, totally cute.

ORIGINAL CAST

Austin Talley (Kyle)
Annie Prichard (Mari)

AUTHOR'S NOTES

A / In between characters dialogue means the NEXT person has started talking; ther e's lots of overlapping.

A nice upscale North-Side Chicago living room of a huge apartment. It's almost fo ur in the

WHERE and WHEN

Morning. Post party. Living Room 3:45 AM

Post-party, pre-crashing. MARI mixes a drink. We hear music from the other room.

KYLE watches, unseen....

KYLE
Did you bring enough for the rest of the party?

MARI
Yes, of course, / I mean totally, totally,

KYLE
What is that? What do you call that?

MARI
Uh, well, / I'm making

KYLE
I mean what are you mixing, what, /would you call that a-

MARI
Well it's actually called a--
It's called a Southern Canadian Encarta.

KYLE and MARI
………………..

KYLE
You're funny.

MARI
But you thought I was serious for a second there, right?

KYLE
Make me one.

MARI
Um. The magic word. Please.

KYLE
You're stealing my liquor from my own party, magic word my ass, make me a drink
.

MARI
---One shot /or two

KYLE
Two.

MARI
Great.

KYLE
Please.

KYLE and MARI
....

MARI makes the drink.

MARI
Do you believe in Scavenger Rights?

KYLE
--Is that like a "Southern / Canadian Thing"

MARI
It's a new thing, it's a now thing, it's like--
So, say you're at a party

KYLE
You are.

MARI
And you don't know a lot of people and you're in a new neighborhood and the host isn't around

KYLE
He is.

MARI
But you're alone, / and it's sosososo_so_ late that you start thinking--

KYLE
You're not.

MARI
Everything's up for grabs. People don't even remember the last names right now, so I, as the most sober person in the /building

KYLE
You're totally not

MARI
As the second most sober person /in the building

KYLE
I'd say eighth or ninth

MARI
As a Survivor of the party--
I have full clearance to become a scavenger. I can grab old bottles, and, loose cigarettes, and it's not stealing--it is a time-honored tradition. Going back centuries. It's a momentary affirmation of--being the last person standing when the fun bomb goes off. Actually, some consider it a badge of honor akin to vigilante justice or the civilian version of the purple heart. I'm basically a hero and all I had to do was steal your booze call it a funny name and make your clean-up tomorrow a little bit less exhausting. I'm basically a saint.
My name's Mari.

KYLE
-Kyle.

MARI
Well. Thanks for having us over. Kyle.

KYLE
You Andy's friend?

MARI
Mark, I know him from work

KYLE
I'm pretty sure Mark sells weed, like, for a living

MARI
Client, supplier, / "work relationships"

KYLE
Uh-huh. Well hey--thanks for coming. You're the last one.

MARI
What about /the couple under the-

KYLE
The couple under the porch moved into the backyard, and then the garage, I think they're in the alley now, which means they're off my property and none of my business.

MARI
Wow. There is nothing hotter then a Chicago asphalt sidewalk in March.

KYLE
Cheers.

They do..........

MARI
Well. Mission accomplished. I / should be

KYLE
Yeah / it's getting late, right?

MARI
Really late, / really really late

KYLE
Here I'll walk you out

MARI
Have a nice-

They kiss.

KYLE
……....I'm not-

MARI
The kind of guy who lures tipsy women into a false sense of security at about 4 in th e morning and then takes them to bed?

KYLE
I'm not.

MARI
Oh fucking shit why the hell not?

KYLE
Because/ I

MARI
It's 4AM.

KYLE
No, no, it's actually / 3:49 AM

MARI
It's basically four in the morning, you're funny, and attractive, and nice, and judgin g by this apartment pretty well off, and you have good music taste, you're great. ….And I'm here.

KYLE
--What if I take you out. Next week.
You know, old fashioned. A date.

MARI
-Do people still do those?

KYLE
We do.
When's the last time you went on one?

MARI
--I don't think in terms of "dates", "Get together", uh--
can't afford to.

KYLE
--Tonight, we can.
All right? " Dream Scenario."

MARI
"Dream Scenario"

KYLE
Absolutely. See, I'll pick you up around /eight

MARI
Pick me up, what do you mean do you have like a like a tandem bike or something?

KYLE
-I drive a car.

MARI
!!!!!!!!!!

KYLE
I pick you up around eight, eight thirty. Friday Night, dressed to the nines, I pick yo u up, we get a drink at Alive One, and then, we go straight to the Green Dolphin

MARI
The Fitness Center?

KYLE
What? No, no, no--honey this is a North Side Night

MARI
I'm from Pilsen

KYLE
I'm sorry about that

MARI
-WHOA

KYLE
Sorry, DREAM / scenario

MARI
Back to the DREAM /scenario, no, it's fine, go, go go

KYLE
(I'm really sorry about that, I am), OK,
Dream Scenario-We're at the Green Dolphin, right, and we're dancing

MARI
You have to ask me I mean not to be anti-feminist I mean it's just polite well I saw i t in a movie once and this is a stupid Dream Scenario I mean shit like this never happens why don't we--

Extends his hand

KYLE
"So. The gentleman offers his hand."

MARI
"I thought you'd never ask."

MARI takes his hand. They move. Slowly, then with pace.

MARI
The Foxtrot

KYLE
Damn right / the foxtrot

MARI
Or the Charleston, can you Charleston?

KYLE
I can even waltz, can you can-can?

MARI
Can you?

KYLE
Can you?

MARI
I can do anything, uh, the Macarena, the dip, /the "vida loca"

KYLE
Whoa whoa, slow down now--
this is a first date

They slow down dancing.

MARI
So we're classy

KYLE
Super classy.

MARY
And it' slow

KYLE
Right, so, so slow

MARI
Right-

KYLE and MARI
Tupac or Biggie?

KYLE
-huh?

MARI
Tupac or Biggie, which one?
When we break out dancing, what's the big song?

KYLE
Why can we only choose one of those two?

MARI
You love em both

KYLE
We're slow /dancing

MARI
But when we speed up again, which one

KYLE
Why's it gotta be hip-hop

MARI
Dip me.

He does.

KYLE
-That's a good first date.

MARI
That's it?

KYLE
That's why /it's a first date

MARI
But then what, what do we do, is there a sequel?

KYLE
Of course there are, relationships go in trilogies--Part One, We dance, Part Two, we dine out-

MARI
OLIVE GARDEN.

KYLE
....WHY THE HELL NOT?!

MARI
I'm getting a bottomless bread stick bowl and I'm bringing tupperware / and boxes

MARI runs to the chips and starts throwing them at KYLE.

KYLE
We eat everything in sight / we take to go boxes and what we don't eat we throw, w e THROW shit!

MARI
FOOD FIGHT!

KYLE
Trashing the place

MARI
OCCUPY / OLIVE GARDEN!

KYLE
OCCUPY OLIVE GARDEN!

They stop throwing shit.

MARI
That's a second date?

KYLE
That's totally a second date, then comes part three

MARI
Part three's always suck, Godfather, Star Wars, Spiderman, recessions-

KYLE
Not this one. Third date? We meet the friends. Your friends, my friends, one room… where'd you go to school?

MARI
Fairfield High, Southern Indiana, Go Tigers.

KYLE
College.

MARI
Didn't go.

KYLE
……….How old are you?

MARI
Old enough to not have a student loan that costs more than my rent.

KYLE
--Just High School?

MARI
Yeah. I mean. You know. I, I checked this website, once? About- about famous p eople who didn't go to college? And apparently there's a lot of people, so, you know, not going to college was was good enough for Andrew Jackson. Henry Ford. You don't have to go to college to, you know, whatever, I mean at the end of the day what's it good for?

KYLE
Describe to me who Henry Ford is.
Or Andrew Jackson.

MARI
……..I /think I need

KYLE
Hey. /Doesn't matter, hey--

MARI
No, actually -

KYLE
Dream Scenario-- We don't need to mix friends. All right, cause it's dangerous, and.....and we can make a new kind of third date.

MARI
...The third one always / sucks

KYLE
Not this time.
We can just walk around the neighborhood, end up at the lake, stay up to late, it's n ot end of the world, it's not make or break this is just a new kind of third date, all right?

MARI
A nice. Long. Walk

KYLE
Neighborhood /to neighborhood

MARI
Just a good old-fashioned stroll

KYLE
Cheaper than a bar

MARI
Cheaper than the green dolphin
KYLE
It's free as we want it to be

MARI
Start in Bridgeport, then go a little more south, /and

KYLE
Rogers Park.

MARI
Oh please, what, are we gonna bring the kids and station wagon? Please.

KYLE
I'd just prefer a neighborhood where I don't have to look over my shoulder every fi ve seconds.

MARI
Oh please, you wouldn't have to,

KYLE
Great, and why's that?

MARI and KYLE
....

MARI
--Know what? I'm --done. Ok. Because the only way this ends is with you accusing me of being a racist /and me having to-

KYLE
I'm sorry, WHAT?!

MARI
Please, you know this is where this is /going

KYLE
Well, sorry, I mean you ask me which rap song we should play and then tell me how I've got nothing to worry about walking around the South Side

MARI
Because IT'S SAFE

KYLE
And of COURSE you would say that because---

MARI and KYLE
....

MARI
I'm getting my bike

KYLE
"Be Careful". All-right?

It's dark out there. White girls in Pilsen. Fixed gears, acting like they own the place, eating Mexican on the weekends and trying to say, "I'm living the life" in Spanish. It'd be funny if it wasn't so fucking embarrassing.
Have a good ride home.

MARI
--Thanks.
It takes me 40 minutes to go from the only place I can afford--
to this shitty little neighborhood, by the lake, where all the black people act like they've moved on up--into what, I don't know.

KYLE and MARI
………………..

KYLE
We never even made it to the third date.
…..Could have just tried it out.

MARI
Or you could have just taken me to bed like a normal person.
But then, of course, how would we both go on living without what just happened.

KYLE
Dream Scenario

MARI
….I'll let myself out.

Holds up the BOTTOM BARREL VODKA.

KYLE
Take the bottle.
…. What'd you call it? A Northern /Fiesta

MARI
"Southern Canadian Encarta."

KYLE
Top Shelf. Keep it.

MARI
Scavenger Rights don't apply to tonight.
….And I know who Andrew Fucking Jackson was.

MARI exits with her BIKE and HELMET. KYLE pours himself a drink.

MUSIC starts. It's slow, a ballad. MARI appears again, sans bike. Lights change.

We're in "The Dream."

KYLE
So, the gentleman offers his hand--

MARI
I thought you'd never ask.

They cross to each other. Just before they start to dance.
Lights Fade.

END OF PLAY

Program B: Echo

BOYS AND VIOLENCE

By Mackenzie Yeager, directed by John Wilson

CHARACTERS
Ben
Andy

ORIGINAL CAST
Roy Gonzalez (Boy 1)
Tim Parker (Boy 2)

AUTHOR NOTE
BEN and ANDY should be played by adult men, but not act like children. They should sound, move and act like adults. They just happen to be seven.

BEN and ANDY, 7, squat on the ground, poking sticks into the dirt.

ANDY
My stomach hurts.

Ben doesn't respond.

BEN
I'm probably allergic to something.

Pause.

Ben pretends to shoot Andy with his finger. Andy shoots back. They resume poking the dirt.

BEN (cont'd)
Let's play Violence.

ANDY
I don't want to play Violence. I want to play videogames.

BEN
(like "no fair")
Uh!

ANDY
It's my house.

BEN
But I'm the guest.

ANDY
Okay, you're right.

BEN
Okay, over here is the jail and that's where the bad guys are. You're the bad guy, General Egregious. Your favorite color is black.

ANDY
(like "no fair")
Uh!

BEN
I'm the guest!

ANDY
Okay.... Can we switch later then?

BEN
Okay.

ANDY
When?

BEN
In like... an hour ten.

ANDY
Okay.

BEN
I'm the Captain. And my men are.... All here. Our colors are red and gold.

ANDY
And you have a giant army that killed my army many moons ago. On another planet.

BEN
Yeah, yeah, yeah!

ANDY
And my colors are actually black and silver, too. Not just black.

BEN
Okay. You killed my wife and children.

ANDY
Cool.

BEN
So I'm getting revenge. Because you killed my wife I had sex with.

ANDY
Did you bring your wife?

Ben takes out a very crumpled piece of a Victoria Secret magazine. He shows it to him.

ANDY (cont'd)
Yeah, she looks like a good wife. I forgot where I put my wife, I'll go look for her.

BEN
No, you're the bad guy. You don't have sex

ANDY
Oh yeah. But I can have sex in an hour ten?

BEN
Yeah, in an hour ten. So you're in jail-

ANDY
I don't want to be in jail!

BEN
I'm the guest!

ANDY
Yeah, but you're not the boss.

BEN
Neither are you.

ANDY
Yeah I am, it's my house, I'm the boss.

BEN
Uh... actually it's your dad's house so he's the boss.

ANDY
Yeah, well if he was here he wouldn't put me in jail.

BEN
But he's not, so we're equal bosses.

ANDY
No...
Andy tries to think of a way around this.

ANDY (cont'd)
Actually God is the boss. If God were here, he'd boss around you, and your dad.

BEN
Well... if you and God were bossing around me and my dad, I'd get Jesus and he would boss around you and your dad and God... The more you know...

ANDY
You're so stupid, Ben. Jesus is God.

BEN
No he's not! Jesus is the supreme ruler!

ANDY
Hah! You're so dumb!

BEN
Everyone knows Jesus has more power than like... all your Magic cards plus mine plus all Yoda's force. He would kill your whole army.

ANDY
God and Jesus are the same, buttrag!

BEN
That doesn't make any sense. If they were the same... then why would Jesus go by "Jesus" when he could go by "God."

Pause.

ANDY
I don't know.

BEN
See?

ANDY
Ben, you don't even go to Sunday school. You don't know any of this.

BEN
Yeah, but my dad has told me about God and church, and he's way smarter than your dad. He has more money. We have a boat.

ANDY
We don't want a boat!

BEN
....Then why do you always ask to come to my boat?

ANDY
Shut up!

BEN
That's a bad word.

ANDY
No it isn't. They say it on Nickelodeon.

BEN
They don't say it on Disney.

ANDY
That's because Disney is for girls. Like you.

BEN
....Take that back.

ANDY
No. You're an idiot girl. You think Jesus is more powerful then God.

BEN
Oh my gosh, God is just God. And Jesus is like Martin Luther King.

ANDY
Jr.

BEN
Yeah yeah Jr. He was a really great guy who walked around and told everyone to be nice to each other, so they killed him. Just like Martin Luther King. Jr.

ANDY
Who's they?

BEN
The bad guys.

ANDY
Oh yeah, I remember that part. But Martin Luther King Jr. was a person, like in history books. But Jesus wasn't just a regular person. He was God's son.

BEN
I thought you said they were the same thing?!

ANDY
I did. But he's also his son. And he tried to tell people that, but the bad guys didn't believe him so they killed him.

Ben does an exasperated thinking pose.

BEN
If Jesus had God's powers... why didn't he just fly away?

Pause.

ANDY
I don't know.

BEN
See!

Ben does a victory dance. Andy watches, getting more and more mad. Andy picks up a stick. He walks over and hits Ben with it, really hard.

BEN (cont'd)
Ouch!

Ben tries to swat the stick away. Andy looks at him for a beat. Then jabs the stick in Ben's eye.

BEN (cont'd)
OUCH! You got my eye! You could scratch my cornea!

ANDY
You're dad is not smarter than my dad.

BEN
(rubbing his eye)
Okay.

ANDY
My dad says your dad's boat is shitty.

He hits Ben again with the stick.

BEN
Stop it!

ANDY
Say your boat is shitty.

BEN
I like our boat.

ANDY
Say it!

Andy goes for him, but Ben tries to fight back with one hand over his eye. They scuffle until Andy has him pinned below him.

BEN
Our boat is shitty!

ANDY
Okay.

Pause. Andy thinks. Then smacks Ben with the stick over and over.

BEN
Why are you doing this?

ANDY
You made me be the bad guy.

Ben rolls into the fetal position, as Andy rolls off the top of him. Ben cries as Andy silently fights invisible soldiers with his stick/sword.

END OF PLAY

SANATORIUM STORY

By Seth Bockley, directed by Lydia Milman Schmidt

CHARACTERS
Kid
Boob/Dad
Pearl/Mom

ORIGINAL CAST
Alexander Allmauger (Child)
Thomas Sparks (Boob/Dad)
Eve Rydberg (Pearl/Mom)

A KID enters.

KID
When I was eight I lived in a TB sanatorium on Fullerton Avenue, by the lake. Sometimes, in the middle of the night, kids would hemorrhage and choke on blood and die. The next day they would cover them with a sheet until someone could take them away. We read funny papers in Color.
One was called Boob McNutt. He was a well-meaning guy but always got into trouble.

BOOB MCNUTT enters. A dapper chap from the 1920's. He bows and clowns a little, like Chaplin.

KID
I read the book of Revelations too, and at night I would get them confused.

KID lies down.

BOOB MCNUTT
If any man worship the beast and his image, and receive his mark in his forehead, he shall be tormented with fire and—

PEARL, BOOB's girl, has entered.

PEARL
Aw, quit your yappin', Boob McNutt. Why I gotta marry an awful boob like you?

BOOB MCNUTT
And the mark of the beast is—

PEARL
Shhh. Boob. Zip it. (*to the KID*)Honey? Honey? Can you hear me? Are you awake?

PEARL and BOOB MCNUTT have become the Kid's MOM and DAD.

MOM
How are you feeling today? Is the cool air doing you any good?

KID
Dad? I had a dream you were Boob McNutt.

MOM and DAD laugh. KID laughs. They all laugh.

DAD
All right, we'll see you tomorrow. Rest well now.
MOM and DAD leave. KID gets up.

KID
On the sixth day, I died, and Boob took me to heaven, which was a candy shop on Diversey that sold big bags of jujubees and Bits-o-honey for a penny apiece.

END OF PLAY

GOODBYE, NIGHT

By Nick Delehanty
With contributions from: Thrisa Hodits, Brandon Ruiter, Hannah Alcorn, Nathan Hulne, Chris Fowler, Nelia Miller, & Pat Coakley

CHARACTERS
Tim
Jimmy
Nate
Lilly
Rob
Tiffany

ORIGINAL CAST
Stephanie Shum (Tiffany)
Chris Fowler (Tim)
Nelia Miller (Margaret)
Partiac Coakley (Jimmy)
Nathan Hulne (Nate)
Brandon Ruiter (Rob)
Hannah Alcom (Lily)

ALL standing in a line outside Alethea, a pharmaceutical manufacturing building holding their belongings (e.g. sleeping bag, backpack). A robotic human voice:

FEMALE ANNOUNCER
Main foyer. Welcome to Alethea. Approximate wait time: 5. Days.

They shuffle to the next station.

FEMALE ANNOUNCER
You are among the first human trials to receive A-2920. If you experience any unpleasant side
effects, please notify one of our on-staff physicians. And the next.

FEMALE ANNOUNCER
Over the course of a lifetime, the average person wastes nearly a quarter million hours sleeping, nearly a third of your life. Approximate wait time: 3. Days.
Morning. The queue room of Alethea. EVERYONE enters the main space with their belongings. TIM, 27, a med student. MARGARET, 22, next to him. JIMMY and Nate are standing together. Tiffany, 27, a visibly pregnant woman is between them and LILLY and ROB.

JIMMY
Fuck no. Absolutely not. You just think you want to live forever.

NATE
That is the most condescending, ridiculous way to answer. It's not even the same thing. This is going to be awesome.

JIMMY
Yes it is. It's what you're chasing. And I want you to admit it.

NATE
What's wrong with wanting more time?

FEMALE ANNOUNCER
Queue Room. Approximate wait time: 1. Day. We appreciate your patience.

LILLY
Oh, thank God.

ROB
Babe! We made it.

TIFFANY
(talking on a cell phone)
We're in.

JIMMY
Remember that time we were driving to San Francisco and we stopped to gamble in Reno?

NATE
Yeah. You pissed away like a month's salary at the Wild Orchid.

JIMMY
No. I invested my money.

NATE
If you consider lap dances from aging strippers an investment, sure.

JIMMY
Best money I ever spent.

TIM studies his note cards, spinning a pen, searching his brain for an answer.

TIM
Shit. Goddamn it.

TIFFANY
It's plasma.

TIM
I have this!

ROB
That seems unlikely.

LILLY
No, one in eight.

ROB
One in eight people die in their sleep?

LILLY
One in eight.

ROB
Well, count us off the list.

LILLY
Not us.

LILLY
Why would we stop? I don't want that time back. They can have it.

ROB and LILLY laugh

JIMMY
I can't remember her name.

NATE
Who?

JIMMY
The stripper.

NATE
I still don't know how you spent all that money. We killed that poker room.

JIMMY
Well, what'd you buy?

NATE thinks. Beat.

Exactly.

NATE
Exactly, what?

JIMMY
I remember what I did with my money. You probably tucked yours away in a savings account.

NATE
Actually, I spent it.

JIMMY
On what?

NATE
A… car payment.

JIMMY makes a scale with his arms.

JIMMY
I knew it. Strippers, Nate. Strippers past their prime who have to work for it. Or a Hyundai. Not even a whole Hyundai. Like two payments on a finance plan.

NATE
I'm pretty close to paying it off.

Evening. TIM sits studying his notecards. TIFFANY is talking on a cell phone.

FEMALE ANNOUNCER
Approximate wait time: 12 hours.

TIM
The ANS regulates... digestion. Heart rate. Respiratory rate. Salivation. Micturition.

flips notecard, realizes he's left one out

Perspiration. Shit.

TIM
Aorta. Pulmonary artery and vein. Right Atrium. Left Atrium. Left ventricle. Right Ventricle. In... Fuck.
In. Inferior...

TIFFANY
(to TIM)
Vena cava.

TIM
Goddamnit, Tiffany.

TIFFANY
(to PHONE)
No. I said no scores under 34. I don't care if she went to Cambridge. Nothing under 34.

TIM
I would have gotten it.

TIM tucks his pen into his shirt.

TIFFANY
(to PHONE)
I just want to read her thesis. I don't think that's too much to ask. You're going to be a father. You should care who's going to teach your daughter phonics.

MARGARET laughs to herself.

ROB
If we leave for Mexico before May, I think I can one bag it.

LILLY
That's perfect. That way I'll have Cyclosporiasis while a bikini.

LILLY takes out a bottle of hand sanitizer and applies it vigorously.

ROB
Do you know how much it costs to check a bag? You might as well buy it a seat. Also, the likelihood of you contracting a waterborne disease is negligible. Drink bottled water. You'll be fine.

LILLY
Oh yeah. Let's just trade microbes for BPAs and phthalates. No. If we go, I'm bringing the Osmosis
system.

ROB
Babe, do you have any idea how much of a pain in the ass it will be to transport an entire reverse /osmosis system?

LILLY
We're bringing it!

MARGARET
My brother's in med school. He never sleeps.

TIM
Hmm? I can't wait to be done with it.

MARGARET
Which one?

TIM
Both I guess. So... I feel like the longer I wait to introduce myself, the more awkward it will be, so for both our sake, I'm just going to do it now.

extending his hand

My name is Tim.

MARGARET
shaking his hand

Margaret Lynn.

TIM
That's Tiffany. She's a horrible monster, pregnant with a future monster.

MARGARET
I wouldn't be here if I were pregnant.

TIM
She's here for the baby. Like, her mother is the head of Ortho at St. Mary's. I can't believe they're going to run trials on an infant. Fucking FDA. Your test scores aren't that high.

TIFFANY
(to PHONE)
I don't care if she hasn't graduated yet. We don't need her for eighteen months.

MARGARET
Why would anyone / do that?

TIM
You know why Asian kids are better at math, right? It's not because they're smarter. Their school days are longer. The brain develops so rapidly in children. They're just further along. Now multiply that by ten.

TIFFANY
No, the math tutor comes after midnight, not the pianist. Do you want to hear her play Greensleeves at 2AM?

TIM
Kid will speak in full sentences before its first birthday.

JIMMY and NATE are playing chess. JIMMY coughs intermittently. LILLY is applying hand sanitizer.

JIMMY
...it's what I'm talking about. The fruit is the whole point of Ms. Pac-Man.

NATE
No, the point is the kill screen. That's how you beat it.

JIMMY
It's not a real end, just the limits of 80s game technology. If it were made now, the game would be

NATE
It can't be infinite. The game would have an end, and eventually someone would get there.

JIMMY
But that's not the point. The point isn't to survive.

NATE
Uh, yeah it is? What does it matter how you win?

JIMMY
I've seen the way you play. It matters.

NATE
Using the power pellets for protection is a legitimate strategy!

JIMMY
Defense!? Fuck de-fense, Man. You'd spend your life on the run? Jesus, no! For ten seconds you're invincible; dude, mouse chases the cat. / It's fucking beautiful.

NATE
That's why you die all the time. You don't even get the extra man.

JIMMY
Jesus Christ. Who gives a shit about the extra man?

NATE
I give a shit. You can't win when you always die for the fruit.

JIMMY
Okay. Imagine you're Ms. Pac-Man. You're husband is dead; eaten by fucking ghosts. Ain't no Mrs. Pac-Man. It's Ms. Pac-Man. She's a widow. You're trapped in their world eating their bland-ass pellets. And all of the sudden a ripe, sweet cherry comes bouncing along. / You're just going to pass that up?!

NATE
The cherry is only worth 100 points.

JIMMY
Holy shit, Nate. Points!?

NATE
Yes, Jimmy. Points. That's how you measure games.

JIMMY
Fuck that. Die for the fruit. Every time.

ROB
Jesus Christ. How'd we get here?

JIMMY
(motioning to NATE)
Dude.

LILLY
You don't care about my safety. You know my body's ecosystem is more delicate than yours.

ROB notices NATE and JIMMY watching the argument.

ROB
Babe, can we not do this here?

LILLY
You put my body at risk and I'm the one who's making a scene?

ROB
I bought the organic stuff.

LILLY
Oh my god. "Made with organic ingredients" is not the same thing as "organic."

ROB
Lillith Rose. I love you, and I/ just want us to move past this.

LILLY
You don't listen.

JIMMY
This is awesome.

TIM
I study twelve hours a day.

MARGARET
That's insane. It's not enough?

TIM
Everyone tries to make it about effort, but it isn't. My Dad always said my brain was made of rubber instead of glue.

MARGARET fights back tears.

TIM
I'm sorry. Did I say something?

MARGARET
No. It's not you. It's nothing.

FEMALE ANNOUNCER
We will be dimming the lights. Enjoy your final night as a slave to sleep.

ROB
This is going to be crazy.

LILLY
No more late nights at the office?

LILLY and ROB lay next to one another.

ROB
Not when I can work anytime. I can't believe this is going to be our last night sleeping next to each other. Have you thought about what you wanted to do with the bedroom?

LILLY
Of course.

ROB
I knew it. Pool table.

LILLY
Absolutely. We can put it in the middle of my walk in closet.

ROB
Should have seen that coming.

LILLY
You're cute. Bikram yoga room.

ROB
So... like a yoga pool table? What are you going to dream about on your last night?

LILLY
I don't know. You don't get to choose your last dream, Silly.

ROB
If you got to pick.

LILLY
I don't know. Smoothies?

ROB
That's your last dream? Smoothies?

LILLY
Mango. With pineapple.

ROB
Not peach?

LILLY
Too many parasites. Mango has tougher skin.

ROB
I'm going to dream about flying.

LILLY
You always dream about flying.

ROB
Because it's amazing. And shockingly difficult. You have to run as fast as you can before you take off. It's exhausting.

TIFFANY
It doesn't matter what you dream about. Just sensory data of no scientific value. Who cares if she dreams of fruit?

EVERYONE
Thank you.

TIFFANY
Shut up.

TIM
Weird to think about that this is our last night of sleep, or dreams.

MARGARET
We can always stop.

TIM
You know your body will catch up on the sleep you missed, right? If you're on it for a couple years and then come off, you're basically be comatose for a year.

MARGARET
I don't care. I like dreaming.

TIM
That's crazy.

MARGARET
I don't want to be here. It's pretty scary. I can't take care of my Dad and work. I figure this way I can do both.

TIM
How long do/ you plan to...

MARGARET
As long as it takes.

TIM
There's no one else who can help?

MARGARET
We didn't have that kind of money. My Dad was a mechanic. I couldn't tell you how many times he borrowed twenty bucks from me. I used to park our Jeep three blocks away so the repo guys couldn't find it.

TIM
That must have been tough.

MARGARET
You get used to it.

TIM
That sounds terrible.

MARGARET
You can get used to anything. It's kinda nice, actually.

TIFFANY
It's called habituation. The human body is incapable of experiencing any stimuli for extended durations of time. It's the body's innate coping mechanism.

JIMMY
She would wreck me in bed. And I would let her.

TIM
(to MARGARET)
Your Dad seems nice.

TIFFANY
Fine.

MARGARET
He was actually kind of a piece of shit.

TIM
Then why help him?

MARGARET
I don't know. Did I hate him for a long time? Yeah. Did my Dad not come home most nights? Sure. But when he did, he'd bring me a Frosty and chicken nuggets.

TIM
It's a fairly transparent bribe.

MARGARET
I know. At least he cared enough to bribe me. To a kid, a Frosty go a long way.

TIM
That's almost sweet.

JIMMY
(To NATE)
I can't believe Leonardo is your favorite ninja turtle. He's such a tool.

NATE
Uh, he's the leader.

JIMMY
Too safe, and careful.

NATE
Who's your / favorite?

JIMMY
Raph.

NATE
Of course you like the brooding / one. Let me ask you this...

TIFFANY
Go to sleep!

MARGARET
Look, I don't want to but I also don't want to have to in the mirror if I don't. But I'm not miserable.

TIM
Neither am I. I'm not.

MARGARET
You're miserable.

TIM
It's just, it's a hard day.

MARGARET
When?

TIM
The day you realize you're bright but not a genius. Hit me my first day of med school.

MARGARET
If you don't want to be there, quit.

TIM
I can't.

MARGARET
Yes you can.

MARGARET takes the note cards from TIM's hands.

MARGARET
Miserable.

TIM
The hard things always do.

MARGARET
No they don't. That's a thing unhappy people say.

TIM picks up the cards.

TIM
I want to understand the circulatory system.

Blackout.
Dawn. TIM and MARGARET are sharing Cliff Bars.
Tiffany is doing mommy yoga. Jimmy is coughing.
LILLY squeezes the last drop from a bottle of hand sanitizer.

FEMALE ANNOUNCER
Good morning. Approximate wait time: 0. Days.

LILLY
I should have brought a mask.

ROB
It really isn't necessary.

LILLY
Like giving me HPV?

ROB
Those were shaving bumps. Doctor Anderson confirmed it. And I have apologized for putting you through that.

LILLY
Should have brought a mask.

ROB
Have I mentioned that I love my wife and that I care deeply about her well-being?

ROB pulls a bio mask from a Ziploc bag in his pocket and hands it to LILLY.
BEAT

LILLY
You are my fantastic. I love you. Thank you.
(To TIFFANY)
Nice down dog.

TIFFANY
I know.

LILLY
Those Lululemon mats are great. Anti-microbial.

TIFFANY
I hate yoga, but it is good for the baby.

LILLY
I could never do yoga pregnant.

TIFFANY
Good for blood flow. It is a common misconception that being sedentary / is beneficial for the fetus, but it is not supported in medical literature.

FEMALE ANNOUNCER
Please proceed to the East entrance. You may dispose of your sleeping bags and pillows.
Everyone except JIMMY gathers their belongings.

NATE
Who needs dreaming? It isn't an essential biological function. It's just something that happens.

JIMMY
How do you know? It could be the whole reason we create art? Maybe all good ideas come from dreams. You willing to just throw it away?

NATE
I dream about taking the garbage out. That isn't the future of art. That's me thinking about garbage.

JIMMY
And what does that say about you!?

NATE
Nothing. It doesn't say anything.

LILLY
Excuse me, gentlemen.

JIMMY
Oh shit. Sorry. Go ahead.

LILLY
Wait, you aren't coming? You waited with us for almost a week?

JIMMY
(to LILLY)
Just trying to talk some sense into to my friend.

JIMMY lets LILLY and ROB in front of him. ROB puts his arm around Lilly.

You're going to love Mexico, Babe.

They exit.

(to NATE)
You're still going through with it.

NATE
Thank you for keeping me company.

JIMMY
Nate.

NATE
I'm sorry you wasted your week.

JIMMY
I don't believe in wasted time. I'll be outside if you change your mind. I hope you do.

NATE hugs JIMMY and exits. JIMMY looks back before exiting through the entrance door.

TIM
Hey, you wanna get coffee sometime?

MARGARET
Doesn't make much sense now.

TIM
Oh. Right. Okay. Never mind.

MARGARET
No, I meant drinking coffee. How about lunch?

TIM
(Pulls out his cell phone)
Sure. Lunch if fine. Lunch is good. I eat lunch.

BEAT
May I have your number?

MARGARET pulls the pen from inside his shirt, and writes her phone number on his hand.

MARGARET
I'm usually off around midnight. You going to be up?

MARGARET exits. The FEMALE ANNOUNCER'S voice comes from the room they entered.

FEMALE ANNOUNCER
Our technicians will be administering your first dose of A-2920. Each pill mimics the biological effects of a full night's sleep. You may receive doses of A-2920 as long as you wish. Should you elect cease your dosage, our facilities will make you comfortable during your
refractory period.

Voice over fades to indistinguishable noise. TIM packs up the last of his belongings and pauses, unsure of which direction to take. He looks at his flashcards on the floor. As the lights fade, the FEMALE ANNOUNCER'S voice is heard again and a new group enters.

FEMALE ANNOUNCER
Queue Room. Approximate wait time: 1. Day. We appreciate your patience.

END OF PLAY

UNTIL THE WORLD IS BEAUTIFUL

By Jack Miggins, directed by Elana Boulos

CHARACTERS
Young Man
Woman

ORIGINAL CAST
featuring William Kiley (Man)
Kristen Magee (Woman)

The young man enters wearing his pack.

Young Man

Hey!

Woman
You're back. That was quick.

Young Man
It was?

Woman
Yeah, you were just down here. The world couldn't have changed that quickly.

Young Man
That was two years ago.

Woman
Huh. Well then, what took you so long?

Young Man
They promoted me. I'm a boss now, so I don't come down this far very often.

Woman
Congratulations.

Young Man
One of the first things I did was stop them from exploring this part of the tunnels. I figured it'd keep you safe for a few... I don't know, decades.

Woman
That's very nice of you. Although, decades...

Young Man
I guess you've seen a lot of them.

Woman
Yeah. I haven't counted in decades in I don't know how long.

Young Man
Have you remembered your name yet?

Woman
Oh. No. I've probably forgotten it even more.

Young Man
Yeah. Anyway, I thought you might be lonely.

Woman
Ha! That's very nice of you.

Young Man
I brought you some stuff from up top.

Woman
You did?

Young Man
It's apple season up there, so I thought you might like one.

He tosses her the apple.

Woman:
Apples. I haven't thought about them in... I don't know.

She throws the apple up and catches it

That sound. That's how you know they're good.

She throws the apple a few more times.

Young Man
Wait 'til you taste it.

The woman bites into the apple. She savors the taste.

Woman
Yeah. That's an apple. Young Man: Good, right? Woman: That is very good. She takes another bite.

Young Man
I thought you might like it. There's more of them up there. Whole trees full. You should come see.

Woman
Nice try.

Young Man
Come on, I'm serious.

Woman
So am I.

Young Man
This is no place for you, down here. Join us. The both of you.

Woman
I'm not here because of apples. The things they did to my family. To me-

Young Man
During the war.

Woman
Yes.

Young Man
But the war's been over for ages.

Woman
But the war wasn't a special occasion.

Young Man
Maybe it was.

Woman
And the people?

Young Man
What about them?

Woman
Do they still hurt each other for no reason?

Young Man
Not for no reason, but yeah, I guess they do.

Woman
And do they cheat each other? Are they cruel? When you're swimming do they grab your shoulder and hold you underwater so they can float?

Young Man
Well, the world is pretty big. There are all kinds of people.

Woman
I'll take that as a yes. It's how we are. But it's not how I am and it's not how he's going to be.

She touches her belly.

But thank you. Ooo. He's kicking.

Young Man
Your little guy?

Woman
Yeah. Do you want to-

\She gestures to her distended belly

Young Man
Can I? I can feel it?

Woman
Just put your hand right here.

She places his hand on her belly. He feels the baby kick.

Young Man
Oh wow. He's really in there.

Woman
Yep.

Young Man
Kicking away.

Woman
Yeah.

Young Man
Is he always pretty active, moving around?

Woman
It comes and goes. Whenever someone finds us he tends to stir. I think it's the voices.

Young Man
Huh. Do you ever think maybe he wants to be born? To be with us?

Woman
I'm sure he does. But if he knew the truth he'd want to stay exactly where he is. I know I would.

Young Man
You sort of already have.

Woman
I guess so.

Young Man
Until the world is beautiful.

Woman
Until the world is beautiful.

Young Man
You're wrong, you know. The world is beautiful. Our Valley, when the sun hits it-

Woman
It's people. What they do. To each other.

Young Man
Well people will always be people. Some are good and some are bad. Or not even; we're all everything. It's just a matter of sorting through it all. Finding the good parts.

Woman
But why? We just have to wait long enough. Young Man: That day will never come.

Woman
We'll just have to see about that.

Young Man
I'm telling you. This is foolish. I can set you up with a house, with a job.

Woman
I can wait.

Young Man
What do you expect to happen?

Woman
But thanks for the apple. I mean it. It's fantastic.

Silence for a little bit.

Young Man
You're welcome. I didn't come down here just to give you an apple, you know.

Woman
Oh?

Young Man
I had a kid.

Woman
You had a baby! Congratulations.

Young Man
Really? That's not what I expected from you.

Woman
Of course. That's wonderful!

Young Man
You don't think it's stupid, given all this?

Woman
No! Life has to go on living. We can't all be down here. I'm just a lucky exception.

Young Man
Oh.

Woman
Is it a boy or a girl?

Young Man
A boy. His name's Vernon.

Woman begins to laugh at the name.

Woman
Vernon. That's a nice name.

Young Man
It was my grandfather's name. It's funny. I'd never seen a baby named Vernon.

Woman
Little Vern.

Young Man
Yeah, but it's made me think of you down here.

Woman
Well it's nice to be thought of.

A moment.

Young Man
When was the last time you laughed?

Woman
Wow. I can't remember.

Young Man
Feels good, doesn't it?

Woman
Yeah, it does. Tell me a joke.

Young Man
Ok... what do you call a fish with no eyes? (Pause) A "FSSH"

The woman laughs.

Woman
That's so stupid.

Young Man
I know. Come up with me.

Woman
No.

Young man
Your boy and Vernon can be friends. We'll show you it's not all bad. Life hurts, yeah. But maybe... maybe-

Woman
Maybe what?

Young Man
Maybe that's how we know the good parts are good.

Woman
I don't think so.

Young Man
I'm telling you you're wrong. Life's hard, what with the planet trying to kill us, and people still do bad things to each other, but should that make me go into hiding for the rest of my life?

Woman
I'm not in hiding. We're in here waiting for a change-

Young Man
Oh, what's the difference? Living's not just not being dead.

He waits for a response. She is silent.

And if a couple thousand years of sitting here with no one but yourself for company hasn't taught you that then I don't quite know what to do. (Pause) I don't know when I'll be back down again, with the family and the job - but I brought you something else.

He takes a wrapped gift out of his pack.

One of my guys found this. I thought you should have it.

She unwraps the gift. It's a boom box.

Woman
What is it?

Young Man
Some kind of music machine. I put in some batteries. We're getting better at making them but they won't last forever. Hopefully it won't take you that long.

Woman
That long to what?

Young Man
To realize it's worth it. To join us. To finally see what he looks like.

Woman
How does it work?

Young Man
Just press this, and it should do the rest.

He presses a button and a song begins playing.

Young Man
(cont.) Good luck. Bye.
They listen to the music for a moment. Young Man turns to leave.

Woman
Wait!

Young Man
What?

Woman
I think I- (she listens to the music a moment longer) Yeah. I remember my name.

Young Man
What is it?

Woman
Agnes.

Young Man
That's a nice name.

Woman
Thank you.

Young Man
What do think you'll name him?

Woman
What's your name?

Young Man
Henry.

Woman
Really?

Young Man
Yes. Why?

Woman
That was my father's name. He was a good man.

Young Man
Was he?

Woman
Yes.

They sit in the silence for a bit.

Young Man
Goodbye, Agnes. I hope I see you soon.

The Young Man leaves. Woman sits in her chair, holding the boom box as the music continues to play. The Woman rises from her seat, looks at the exit. She sits back down, hugs the boom box, and continues to listen. The music plays as lights fall on

Agnes, *waiting.*

TOMORROW

By Caitlin Parish, directed by Josh Sobel

CHARACTERS
Man

ORIGINAL CAST
Eric Roach (Man)

MAN
The sun'll come out tomorrow. Or not. Actually, not. The sun will not come out tomorrow. Please keep your bottom dollars.

You see, the sun's been reading a great deal lately. Theory, mostly. A mid-life hobby to fill the quiet hours. Got around to Heisenberg last week, and hit the Uncertainty Principle. And, lemme tell you, heavenly bodies are very thrown by the idea that there's only so much we can know about our position and momentum in life. Heavenly bodies feel a certain sense of entitlement and permanence. They're been doing what they do for an awfully long time, and frankly, the idea of that ending is unsettling. Our sun, though, took this opportunity to do some self-examination. Should it embrace uncertainty? It's been the sun for 4.5 billion years, and if it doesn't try to do something new with its life now, well... its not getting any younger. Next thing it knows it'll have gotten big around the middle and start feeling an unpleasant grind right at the core and no one will gaze adoringly at the unsightly planetary nebulas popping up all over its now loose and wrinkly outer layer. And from there its just a hop, skip, and a jump until its a white dwarf puttering around a cooling solar system with distant kids and a sense that this could be a lingering, lonely end.

So, the sun will not be coming out tomorrow. Or up. It will not be darkest before the dawn. It will be darkest before the totally black. The forecast will be dark with a light smattering of dark. The sun will be taking some “me time”.

Of course, like all moments of necessary selfishness, there will be consequences. I'm not even talking about us. We'll, you know...we'll be okay. We'll have a sweet eight minutes before the light completely fades, a week before the surface temperature dips to 0 degrees, a month before it hits negative 100. Layers will be very in this summer. And I have good news for Iceland! Since you already heat most of your homes harnessing geothermal energy from subterranean volcanoes, you can kind of keep doing that. In a post-economy world, you will reign supreme: blonde and cozy and worshiping your pixie goddess Bjork.
We'll be fine. But there will be personal consequences. Tomorrow morning...well, funny thing about the word “morning.” Sort of contingent on the sun coming up, so... we'll have to come up with a name for what that time will be. “Morning” from the Middle English morwen, but also possibly the proto-Indo- European root mergh which meant blink...Tomorrow blinking the sun will creep out of bed slowly, subverting its blinking, numbed routine. It will slip on a pair of comfortable shoes, take a lot of cash, and head for the door, hoping not to wake anyone.

But that's when the sun will hear, “Where do you think you're going?” Of course this would be the first time in years that the moon wasn't working late. Although, the sun's gotta be honest with itself, it doesn't really know what the Moon gets up to at night. For all the sun knows the Moon could be fucking around with that dickbag comet Halley, who always seems to be coming into town for short business trips.

The sun made peace with that a long, long time ago, but Christ, the sun was hoping it could leave without a scene.

But the sun turns, and there's the moon. And, man, the moon looks good. 4.4 billion years old but doesn't look a day over 4.2. Putting on weight again, thank God. Pale, with those cheek bones, and tired. And the moon's just staring: at the shoes, the pockets bulging with cash, the open door.

"Where are you going?"

The sun doesn't know what to say. What can it say? That it's tired of being the only one to generate light. That it finds itself staring at planets barely older than Earth and wondering what they're like in orbit. That every time the moon falls into its regular fear that it's old, and tries everything it can to be new, all the sun sees is someone empty and shadowed. That the moon is cold to the touch.

The sun doesn't have to say it. The moon's always known that the sun would take this road. But yesterday the moon didn't know that it would be tomorrow. Which is now today.

Somewhere along the way, the pair of them stopped questioning. They fell into their own spins and went with what worked. Lots of things seemed very important.
"Where are you going?" "Just for a walk."
The moon has never really put stock in a higher power, but it feels downright Biblical. It feels like it might turn to blood, like it might cleave in half and leak mountains. It knows full well that it's been drifting further and further away of its own accord, but it never imagined that the sun would be the one to walk out.

What'll happen to it if the sun goes? Sure, the moon will exist, but no one will look at it anymore, and as far as the moon is concerned, going through life unseen is worse than death.

It's so stupid, but they're both thinking about their first date. It was an accident. They were both at the same bash, packed wall to wall with all these bright young things. They both turned into the same quiet corner, looking for a breath of air, and saw...wow. When they looked at each other, it was like being seen for the first time. The sun hadn't known it could heat. The moon hadn't known it could glow. They looked and saw the future, saw little round beings running around. They revolved around each other. They started to dance.

But now they're looking at each other and there's no warmth. There's no shine. There's a long line of yesterdays, and days when promises were made, and tomorrows when they were broken. And it's not just one individual's fault. The day comes when there's no tomorrow, there's just the day something has to end.
The sun has gone for a walk with no particular destination. The moon won't be coming out tomorrow either. It's hiding upstairs so we won't know it's drinking.

Earth is alone now. It'll go on, a little colder. Harder. The sun will not be coming out tomorrow. Or maybe it will.

Maybe tomorrow the moon moves in close, and hums, and they remember why they started dancing in the first place. Maybe the sun presses its forehead against the moon's deep, cool collarbone, and gets some rest. Maybe we will all fly above the obstacles we believe paramount. The figures we long for will appear before us. We will put our arms around light. And light will take us in its arms. Maybe.
But the certainty about tomorrow is that it's the great uncertainty. That's the mystery, and the hope, and the gift.
Please plan accordingly.

BASED ON A TRUE STORY

By Usman Aly, directed Sonny Das

CHARACTERS
ISMAIL American of Jordanian descent. 30.
JAKE White American. 30s. Friendly face.
JESUS (haysoos) Puerto Rican American. 30s. Clean-shaven. Big. Intimidating.

ORIGONAL CAST
Anant Sharma (Ismael)
Armando Reyes (Jesus)
Damian Conrad (Jake)

SETTING
Chicago Apartment.

TIME
2013

LIGHTS COME UP to a Chicago apartment. There is a couch, coffee table, and a big screen TV.

ISMAIL enters from another room, putting his coat on while on the phone.

ISMAIL
Ok, Yeah, I'll buzz you guys up. One sec.

ISMAIL heads to the door, presses the buzzer.

ISMAIL
Yeah, did it open? Here, I'll do it again. Okay good. See you soon.

ISMAIL puts a few things away, tidies up a bit. KNOCK ON DOOR. He answers

ISMAIL
Hey! Come on in.

Both bundled up in a lot of winter clothing. Big, heavy jackets. Cold out. Jake has had a drink or two already. Maybe has one with him, hidden.

JAKE
Oh shit, it's cold out man. Hey. Thanks. Fuck. Shit.

ISMAIL
Yeah, if you guys could take your shoes off.

JAKE
No sweat.

They begin to do so. but just their shoes.

ISMAIL
Hey, I'm Ismail.

JAKE
Oh, sorry man. Jesus, this is Ismail. Ismail this is Jesus.

JESUS (hay-soos)
Hey bro.

ISMAIL
Hey.

JAKE
Thanks for letting us use your place man.

JESUS
Yes, thank you.

ISMAIL
It's fine...it's just the two of you right?

JAKE
Yup.

ISMAIL (needs to leave)
Okay cool. Well the TV is there

JESUS
Huge!

JAKE
Told you.

ISMAIL
You guys make yourselves at home. Kitchen in the back, bathroom upstairs. Jake knows.

JAKE
Yup.

JESUS
Seriously man, thanks for letting us into your home to watch the game.

JAKE
You're the only person I know with the package.

JESUS (noticing the channels)
Super cable.

ISMAIL
It's cool.

JESUS
Are you gonna stick around to watch?

ISMAIL
No, I gotta run. Plus I don't really have a dog in this-

JESUS
I know, it's different right? How many guys you know still watch High School Football?

ISMAIL
Seems like it means a lot to Jake-

JESUS
And me. We're from the same area in California-

ISMAIL
You guys went to high school together?

JESUS
Oh no! Rival schools.

JAKE
It's like religion where we grew up.

ISMAIL
Nice. Well I'm gonna run-

JESUS
No high school football back home?

ISMAIL
In India? No-

JESUS
Guess it's an American thing huh?

ISMAIL
Seems like it. Okay, I'm gone. I'll be back in a couple of hours. Have fun. Don't trash the place.

JAKE (pulling out some beers)
We won't!

ISMAIL
I'm just gonna-

As ISMAIL begins to leave, JESUS starts taking his coat off. We see that under his coat he is wearing stereotypically Arab garb. He pulls on a turban from his bag, a fake beard, and puts it on. Sits down on a "magic carpet", pops open a beer. Starts watching TV.

ISMAIL
Um-

JAKE
Oh. I know, pretty awesome right?

JAKE then takes off his coat to reveal he is wearing a dothi. He sits down, and places a bhindi on his forehead. They drink. ISMAIL speechless.

JESUS (to Jake)
Ah! You fucking Paki! Game should be on soon.

JAKE
You're gonna get killed A-Rab.

LONG SILENCE as ISMAIL takes this all in.

JAKE
Have fun tonight man. And thanks again!

MORE SILENCE. They eat chips, and drink

ISMAIL
Hey guys.

JAKE/JESUS
Yeah?

ISMAIL
Why are you dressed like that?

BEAT

JAKE
Oh dude! Haha! Sorry, school mascots.

ISMAIL
What?

JESUS
Coachella Valley High Arabs!!

JAKE
Indio High Indians!!

JESUS
Kill the Indians! A-R-A-B-S!

PAUSE

ISMAIL
Your...your mascots are the Arabs and the Indians.

JESUS
Yup.

JAKE
It's all fun man. Everyone dresses up. Cheers on their team. We dig it.

JESUS
It's super positive.

ISMAIL
You don't feel strange...as a latino?

JESUS
No dude. I mean, do you have a problem with the Redskins?

ISMAIL
Well-

JESUS
Exactly. It's just sports.

ISMAIL
Okay. Whatever. I'll see you guys later.

JAKE
Have fun!

ISMAIL (takes it in one last time, then)
America. Weird fucking place.

ISMAIL tries to head out the door.

JESUS
What was that?

ISMAIL
Sorry?

JESUS
What did you say?

ISMAIL
Nothing.

JESUS
I don't think so.

JESUS stands up. Goes towards him. Still in full garb.

JESUS(Continued)
What's so weird about America?

Jesus is genuinely offended

JESUS
Well?

JAKE
Okay easy now.

ISMAIL
Um. This. This is what's weird about America.

JAKE
We're supporting our teams bro.

ISMAIL
I'm sorry, but why are your teams called the Indians and the Arabs-

FROM THE TV, we hear "And here come the Coachella High Arabs"

ISMAIL
And your mascot looks like...Osama Bin Laden

JESUS
Watch it man.

ISMAIL
Whatever. Just watch your game. I can't pretend to understand this-

JESUS
Well maybe you should learn. High School football is like religion man.

ISMAIL
I know, I tried to watch Friday Night Lights-

JESUS
Then you should get it-

ISMAIL
And I hated it.

JAKE
FUCK! No one hates Friday Night Lights!!

JESUS
No one! I feel uncomfortable being here.

ISMAIL
Look I'm gonna drop it okay. It's fine.

JESUS
Um yeah, actually bro, it's not fine.

JAKE
Easy A-rab!

JESUS
No, no easy.

ISMAIL
What's not fine?

JESUS
It's. Not. Fine.

ISMAIL
To have a difference of opinion?

JESUS
You think this is racist or something?

ISMAIL
Wellll

JESUS
You think it's "xenophobic" or "jingoistic"-

JAKE
It's not! It's football!

JESUS
Or maybe you think it's disrespectful-
JAKE
Football!!

ISMAIL
Why is this escalating so fast-

JESUS
You think that? You think I'm not aware of racial stereotyping? I'm latino man!

ISMAIL
Exactly.

JESUS
It's pride. I'm a proud Arab.

ISMAIL
No, you're not. You just said you're-

JAKE (Indian accent)
I'm a proud Indian!

JESUS
Do you know that Coachella has a history of Arab influence?

ISMAIL
No but-

JAKE
Listen. Learn.

JESUS
We have towns in our area of California called Mecca and Medina. Arab traders came to our part of America, and planted dates.

JAKE
They export dates man!

JESUS
We have belly dancers at our games.

JAKE
Sexy ones!

JESUS
And when they come out on the field? What? You think we boo? You think we hiss or say some bad shit about the Arab belly dancer? Call her a sand nigger or something?

ISMAIL
No-

JESUS
That's right! We cheer. We aren't racist. We cheer the belly dancer. We cheer the magic carpet ride!

JAKE
We have lots of IT specialists in our town!

JESUS
That's no xenophobia-

JAKE
That's why we're the Indians!

JESUS
That's respect. Celebrating the culture of our part of California. And celebrating football.

ISMAIL
Okay man. I gotta go.

JESUS
You still haven't told me why you said that.

ISMAIL
Said what?

JESUS
Don't play with me man-

ISMAIL
I'm sorry, but I'm having a hard time taking you seriously dressed like that-

JESUS
See, now that's racist-

ISMAIL.
No, what you are wearing is racist. And you, Jake.

JAKE (hurt)
Me? But I'm friends with you. I can't be racist. I think your sister's hot. I'm like the opposite of racist.

ISMAIL (ignoring him)
I stick by it, America is a weird place.

JESUS
You can have your opinions on football and you can have your opinions on me, even though you just met me, but I don't think you have the right to bash America.

ISMAIL
Who's bashing America?

JESUS
You are!

JAKE
He has a point.

ISMAIL
Jake you need to control your friend, or you guys can11.

JAKE
Just listen to him. Don't be so close-minded!

JESUS
I love this country, and this is my home. Yeah, we have our issues but it's still the greatest country in the world.

ISMAIL
Oh boy.

JESUS
The best country in the world. I voted for Obama. A black man. Where else in the world can you vote for a black man as President?

ISMAIL
Um, all of Africa-

JAKE
Nowhere. Nowhere else.

JESUS
And even if you think that this is racist-

JAKE
Which it isn't-

JESUS
Don't act like it's uniquely American.

ISMAIL (gathering himself)
Look man. I'm not saying America is the only place where people can be racist. All I said was America is weird-

JESUS
Unique!

JAKE
Exceptional!

ISMAIL
It's fucking weird. You guys are fucking weird right now. Your nationalistic sentiment is weird. The way race and ethnicity manifest in the world of Sports mascots, the obsession with High School Football, all of this is uniquely American, and uniquely WEIRD. It doesn't happen anywhere in the world but here. Liverpool aren't the Chinamen, Manchester United aren't the Micks-

JAKE
But soccer is way gay-

JESUS
They have racist hooligans-

ISMAIL
That's not my point-

JESUS (incredulous)
They throw bananas at black players!

ISMAIL
That is not my point-

JESUS
Don't bash America man.

ISMAIL (exasperated)
I don't even know why I'm getting into this. I should just ask you to leave.

JESUS
Fuck you. Pussy.

BEAT

ISMAIL
Excuse me.

JESUS
I'm not going anywhere. Neither are you.

ISMAIL
Jake?

JAKE
Fuck bro. He's fucking right Ismail. We're not leaving. Cancel your plans. This is for your own good.

ISMAIL (sensing the danger)
Guys...Look I'm sorry, I just…

JESUS (approaching)
The reason you feel this way, the reason you wanna bash America is because you're ignorant. You see color everywhere. You see prejudice everywhere.

JAKE
Like Jews.

JESUS
You can't even see that when I dress like this, when Jake dresses like that, we are celebrating where we come from. Our culture. Our heritage.

JAKE
This is the 21st century. There is a black man in office. Change has come. Stop trying to divide everyone.

ISMAIL (pushed down on the couch)
Guys-

JAKE
You need to learn how to be an American, Ismail.

ISMAIL
I am an American.

JAKE
On paper sure. But you need to learn how to BE American.

They sit down next to him. Flanking him.

ISMAIL
What are you doing?

JESUS
You're gonna watch the game with us.

JESUS
Have a beer

Jake gives him one.

JESUS
Drink it. America. You can love it or leave it.

JAKE
What's it gonna be?

ISMAIL
....

JAKE
Love it.

JESUS
Yeah, you are.

He clinks his beer with Ismail's.

JESUS (puts his headdress on Ismail's head.)
Learn. Embrace it. Now let's go A-rabs. Right?

JAKE and JESUS stare at ISMAIL. Ismail looks at the TV screen.

ISMAIL
Right.

BLACKOUT.
END OF PLAY

THE RISE AND FALL OF EVERYTHING IN THE WORLD

The Rise and the Fall by Brook Allen, directed by Diana Raselis

CHARACTERS
X
Y

ORIGINAL CAST
Daniela Colucci (X)
Alex Stein (Y)

X and Y they sit in the dark

X
It's rather dark in here, isn't it?

Y
No.

X
What do you mean, no?

Y
I mean, I'm not sure. What is "dark"?

X
The opposite of light.

Y
I see.

X
Impossible. Here, perhaps I can just…

Sounds of X fiddling around in the dark, he mumbles to himself. Finally he turns on a hanging light. It swings above them. They both stare at it, following its swings.

Y
Whoa.

Looking at his own hands for the first time

WHOA.

Sees X and touches his face

WHOA!

X
Maybe some sound?

Y
That might be nice. I enjoy a nice sound now and then.

X runs offstage and quickly returns with a drum which he lightly beats. X and Y groove for a minute. X hands the drum over to Y who continues playing.

X
Do you think I should make others?

Y
Other whats?

X
Other us-es

Y
How? We are the only us-es there are, and we're right here so…

X waves his hand the hanging light raises up, revealing the audience.

X/Y
Whooooooa.

X and Y head directly into the audience and invade all kinds of personal space. Touching people's faces and hair etc.

X
I think I can make ANYTHING.

Y
If you can make anything, does that mean you can make everything?

X
I think I can create EVERYTHING.

Y
That sounds so /dangerous

X
/fabulous.

Y
Don't create anything else.

X
Why?

Y
Because. This is nice how it is. Just like this. Don't, you know, mess with it.

X
Maybe just one more thing?

Y
Last thing?

X
Last thing.

Y
Ok, fine.

X runs offstage and returns pulling, with all of his might, a giant rope tied to a tiny red wagon. Strapped to the wagon tall and bulging, is everything in the world.

X
So maybe it's two more things. A few more things. Fine, it's all the things. But they're important! Look!

He plucks items from the wagon and wildly throws them into the audience

Air! Water! Land! Clocks! Schedules! Animals! Diseases! Ambition! Pop Tarts! Electricity! Etc.

While X is celebrating his creations, Y has climbed to the top of the pile on the wagon and is reaching for the light. X winds down eventually, exhausted.

X (cont'd)
Glaciers! Pollution! Internet! Bi-Polar Disorder! Ice Cream! (Winded, beat) Now you.

Y
Me what?

X
See if you can make anything more wonderful than all of this.
Y
Ok, how about this?

Y leans over to the hanging light, stares at it a moment, smiles, then turns it off.

END OF PLAY

10 THINGS

By Scott Tobin, directed by Emmi Hilger

CHARACTERS

PAUL (as age 10 through 80)

ORIGINAL CAST

Scott Ray Merchant (Man)

LIGHTS UP. THERE ARE EIGHT CHAIRS ACROSS THE LENGTH OF THE STAGE, SPREAD APART BY ABOUT A FOOT AND IN A SMALL SEMI CIRCLE. PAUL, AS AGE 10, IS IN THE FIRST CHAIR.

PAUL (as age 10)
Thank you God for these following ten things: 1) the wagon, 2) the new Xbox game, 3) passing Math class, 4) that tomorrow is Saturday, 5) that it is almost summer break, 6) that my mom left the string beans in the supermarket by mistake, 7) that I got to see that boobie on TV before I got sent out of the room, 8) that my dog just missed getting hit by that car, 9) that the Jets won and 10) my parents, I love them.

LIGHT CROSSFADE AS PAUL SWITHCES TO THE SECOND CHAIR.

PAUL (as age 20)
Thank you God for these following ten things: 1) the car for graduation, 2) the new PlayStation game, 3) passing physics, 4) the party tonight, 5) that it's almost the summer, 6) that Hot Pockets are so cheap, 7) Moira Stanton, 8) that my roommate will be gone for two weeks 9) that the Jets won and 10) my Mom, I love my Mom.

LIGHTS CROSSFADE AS PAUL SWITHCES TO THE THIRD CHAIR.

PAUL (as age 30)
Thank you God for these following ten things: 1) that my car repairs are under $500, 2) updated Microsoft, 3) the quarterly numbers, 4) free dinner at the event tonight, 5) the summer rental, 6) Sriracha sauce, 7) porn star Emma Mae, 8) that Moira will be gone for the weekend, 9) that the Jets won and 10) my Mom, I love my Mom.

LIGHTS CROSSFADE AS PAUL SWITHCES TO THE FOURTH CHAIR.

PAUL (as age 40)
Thank you God for these following ten things: 1) the town car to and from work, 2) IPad, 3) my bonus, 4) my bonus, 5) four weeks of vacation, 6) take out, 7) Melissa Crane, 8) the end of alimony, 9) that the Jets won and 10) my Mom, I must visit my Mom.

LIGHTS CROSSFADE AS PAUL SWITCHES TO THE FIFTH CHAIR.

PAUL (as age 50)
Thank you God for these following ten things: 1) Finally, the Lexus, 2) Ms. Pac Man, 3) sold the stock just in time, 4) health insurance, 5) Christmas at a restaurant, 6) the new James Patterson book, 7) sleeping pills, 8) my journal, 9) that the Jets won and 10) that my Mom went peacefully in her sleep.

LIGHTS CROSSFADE AS PAUL SWITHCES TO THE SIXTH CHAIR.

PAUL (as age 60)
Thank you God for these following ten things: 1) new Nike's, 2) the big book of Word Search, 3) the interest, 4) the surgery went ok, 5) Thai food delivery, 6) Simpsons DVD gift set box, 7) the few hours of sleep last night, 8) that Moira's second husband made it through, 9) that the Jets won…

He waits a moment and skips saying the number 10 this time.

PAUL (as age 60)
I miss my mother very much…

LIGHTS CROSSFADE AS PAUL SWITCHES TO THE SEVENTH CHAIR.

PAUL (as age 70)
Thank you God for these following ten things: 1) stopping the pain, if only for a few minutes, 2) the lovely painting of the deer in the woods, 3) the walk in the lovely weather today, 4) the surgery went ok, 5) pizza!, 6) the lovely retirement party, 7) the new mattress delivery, 8) the call from Moira, it's been so many years, 9) that the Jets won, 10) that picture I found of my mother. She looked so young…so young.

LIGHTS CROSSFADE AS PAUL SWITCHES TO THE EIGHTH CHAIR.

PAUL, AS 80, SITS THERE, ALONE, STARING OUT. HIS EXPRESSIONS SHOW THAT HE IS THINKING HARD AND REMEMBERING SOME OLDER TIMES. AFTER LOOKING FRUSTRATED FOR A BIT, HE FINALLY SMILES.

FADE LIGHTS.

END OF PLAY

www.ingramcontent.com/pod-product-compliance
Ingram Content Group UK Ltd.
Pitfield, Milton Keynes, MK11 3LW, UK
UKHW041942190726
13854UKWH00004B/1749

9 781312 247383